The OTHER Teachers

For Dusty, thank you for being a friend.

The OTHER Teachers

A Guide to Psychological Safety Among Educators

Ricky Robertson

For information:

Corwin
A Sage Company
2455 Teller Road
Thousand Oaks, California 91320
(800) 233-9936
www.corwin.com

Sage Publications Ltd.
1 Oliver's Yard
55 City Road
London, EC1Y 1SP
United Kingdom

Sage Publications India Pvt. Ltd.
Unit No 323-333, Third Floor, F-Block
International Trade Tower Nehru Place
New Delhi 110 019
India

Sage Publications Asia-Pacific Pte. Ltd.
18 Cross Street #10-10/11/12
China Square Central
Singapore 048423

Vice President and Editorial Director: Monica Eckman
Publisher: Jessica Allan
Content Development Editor: Mia Rodriguez
Content Development Manager: Lucas Schleicher
Senior Editorial Assistant: Natalie Delpino
Production Editor: Vijayakumar
Copy Editor: Pam Schroeder
Typesetter: TNQ Tech Pvt. Ltd.
Proofreader: Girish Sharma
Indexer: TNQ Tech Pvt. Ltd.
Cover Designer: Gail Buschman
Marketing Manager: Olivia Bartlett

Printed and bound by CPI Group (UK) Ltd, Croydon, CR0 4YY

Library of Congress Cataloging-in-Publication Data

Names: Robertson, Ricky, author.

Title: The other teachers : a guide to psychological safety among educators / Ricky Robertson.

Description: Thousand Oaks, California : Corwin Press, [2025] | Includes bibliographical references and index.

Identifiers: LCCN 2024035827 | ISBN 9781071921081 (paperback) | ISBN 9781071921128 (adobe pdf) | ISBN 9781071921098 (epub) | ISBN 9781071921111 (epub)

Subjects: LCSH: Teachers–Professional relationships. | Teachers–Psychology. | Mentoring in education. | Teaching–Pyschological aspects.

Classification: LCC LB1775.R563 2025 | DDC 371.102/3–dc23/eng/20240812

LC record available at https://lccn.loc.gov/2024035827

This book is printed on acid-free paper.

25 26 27 28 29 10 9 8 7 6 5 4 3 2 1

CONTENTS

ACKNOWLEDGMENTS

First and foremost, many thanks to the educators whose stories inspired this book. Thank you for taking the time to share your experiences with me. I trust that your contributions will help create psychologically safe schools.

Writing is a challenging, laborious, and transformative process for me. I could not have written this book without the support and encouragement of my family and my dear friends, especially my mom, Beth, Faith, Jesse, Zach, Nick, Richard, Ernie, Doreen, Dan, Jamil, and Gabriel. I am thankful for your love.

Last, thank you Jessica Allan, my editor, and the wonderful publishing team at Corwin. Your guidance and patience helped me conquer my inner critic and get words on the page.

Publishers Acknowledgments:

Kara Proctor-Dunn
School Counselor
Woodbridge, VA

Meghan Love, M.Ed.
ESOL teacher
Fort Mill, SC

Rebecca Cohen
School Counselor
Portland, OR

Amanda Austin
School Counselor
Portland, OR

ABOUT THE AUTHOR

Ricky Robertson is an educator, author, and consultant. He has had the privilege to work with students from pre-K to 12th grade who have persevered in the face of adversity and trauma. He began his career in education as a New York City public high school teacher, teaching in one of the city's highest-performing public schools. He then went on to work as a teacher, behavior specialist, and, eventually, as an administrator in traditional and alternative schools supporting students with significant mental health and behavioral needs.

Ricky is the coauthor, along with Victoria Romero and Amber Warner, of the Corwin best-selling book *Building Resilience in Students Impacted by Adverse Childhood Experiences: A Whole Staff Approach*. The model that he and his coauthors developed in their book was included in the *Roadmap for Resilience: The California Surgeon General's Report on Adverse Childhood Experiences, Toxic Stress, & Health* as an example of best practices for schools to support children and families affected by toxic stress and trauma. Robertson continues to work with state and federal policymakers as an adviser on trauma-informed care in public health and education policy.

As a consultant and coach, Robertson works with schools, school districts, education service districts, and state departments of education across the country to develop systems of support that foster achievement, well-being, and resilience among staff and students. His work has been featured in podcasts, online media, books, magazines, national conferences, as well as a trauma-informed teaching video series developed by the National Education Association, WETA, and AdLit.

Ricky finds inspiration in the resilience of young people and the heart and hard work of educators.

INTRODUCTION

Psychological safety in the workplace is a shared belief that it is safe for us to ask questions, express concerns, try new strategies, and challenge the status quo without fear of humiliation, punishment, or retaliation from colleagues. Psychological safety has been shown to have a significant influence on how happy we are at work and how effectively we collaborate with our colleagues. Yet, when I started writing this book there were not any books available that focused on psychological safety among K–12 educators. At that time, most of the research and resources explored the topic within corporate settings, health care, and a variety of other fields, but little attention was paid to how psychological safety develops within schools. Educators face unique challenges and considerations when it comes to creating psychologically safe teams and work environments.

After reviewing the research and familiarizing myself with the work of psychological safety thought leaders, such as Amy Edmondson and Timothy Clark, I turned to my fellow educators as a primary source of insight. As a consultant and coach, I have the honor to work with educators across the country and beyond. In the years leading up to the publication of this book, I invited educators to share their experiences of working in psychologically safe as well as psychologically unsafe schools. I spoke with educators who taught in urban, suburban, and rural communities; in private, public, and charter schools; and across grade levels, content areas, and departments. Their stories informed the topics you will read about in this book, ranging from painful experiences of workplace bullying to inspiring journeys of transformation and collective efficacy.

Although this book is titled *The Other Teachers*, any professional who works in schools may find it to be a helpful resource. The stories contained in these chapters were also inspired by interviews I conducted with superintendents, district administrators, school principals, paraprofessionals, school counselors, school psychologists, and education support professionals. Regardless of your professional role, know that each individual influences the psychological safety of their school. When staff members and leadership work together to cultivate and sustain a more psychologically safe school, all members of the school community benefit.

I've been fortunate enough to assist schools in their efforts to develop psychological safety among staff and seen firsthand the positive effects this work has on reducing burnout, strengthening collaboration, and improving student outcomes. As you will learn in this book, there is no one-size-fits-all approach to creating a psychologically safe environment for staff, students, and families because each school community is unique. However, we will explore stages of psychological safety that provide insight into the ways our relationships, teams, and school culture can foster greater belonging, trust, and impact.

This book is not complete without you. As you read this book, I invite you to engage with the reflection questions and add your own insights to the key takeaways, strategies, practices, and tools. My hope is that this book enhances your awareness, knowledge, insight, skill, and ability to nurture psychologically safe relationships with your colleagues. May you and your colleagues create schools where everyone feels included, inspired to learn, appreciated for their hard work, and mutually supported through teamwork.

CREATING PSYCHOLOGICALLY SAFE SCHOOLS FOR EDUCATORS

I was walking to my car after a professional development workshop on trauma-informed teaching that I had facilitated for a large suburban high school when one of the teachers approached me. I could tell from the tension in her face that what she was about to share with me pained her in some way. She looked around to make sure that no one was within earshot and said in a quiet voice, "For me, the most difficult thing about teaching isn't the students; it's the other teachers."

She went on, "There's so much gossip, blame, and criticism among the staff here. You're either part of the in crowd that has a say in all the decisions, or you're in the out crowd that the administration ignores. This school is run by cliques. We teach high school, but we're worse than the students." What this teacher could not have known was that I had heard similar sentiments voiced by countless educators across the country, educators who love what they do but find that their interactions with colleagues often add stress to their already demanding jobs. As educators, we anticipate that we'll encounter students who may be occasionally disrespectful, but many of us find ourselves surprised and deeply hurt when we feel disrespected, judged, overlooked, or even excluded by our colleagues.

For educators who find themselves in toxic school environments, we may attempt to buffer social stressors at work by isolating or by finding a colleague (or if we're lucky a small group of coworkers) with whom we connect and can vent to when work gets to be too much. Finding your people is healthy. It becomes a problem only when educators feel forced to choose between being a lone soldier or joining a pack to navigate the negativity and drama within their school. When this happens, the staff fragments, and dysfunctional dynamics become entrenched, eroding the possibility of effective collaboration.

Some of you may be fortunate enough to work in schools where you feel valued and supported. In healthy, resilient schools, educators know that they are part of a team. They recognize that each student is everyone's student. These educators don't face challenges alone because their team has their back, and their students receive greater support as a result. However, many educators do not have this experience. They carry the burden of this profession largely on their own shoulders. Asking for help, attempting new strategies, or being courageous enough to advocate for positive change comes at a cost. They may encounter criticism, backlash, and backstabbing when they risk authenticity or innovation within a toxic workplace culture. The ways that we treat one another at work have a significant impact on our mental health as well as our career satisfaction and performance. Schools are safe and healthy places for students only when they are safe and healthy places for educators.

PSYCHOLOGICAL SAFETY

The purpose of this book is to assist educators in creating schools where they feel connected, valued, supported, and inspired. This requires us to investigate the nature of harmful workplace dynamics and determine what we can do to transform them. To aid us in this journey, we will consider stories based on the real-life experiences of educators from around the country as well as research on creating psychologically safe workplaces.

Some of the stories included in this book may evoke painful feelings because they describe ways that we inadvertently and, at times, intentionally harm one another during a typical school day. These depictions may trigger negative memories or emotions connected to similar experiences you have had or are currently experiencing. If this happens, please be gentle with yourself. Feel free to set this book aside and practice some small act of self-care. You may decide to take a few deep breaths, stretch, journal about your feelings, or quit your job. I am kidding about the last suggestion, sort of. We will hear from an educator later in the book whose transfer to another school was her last and only available solution. In her case, self-preservation was the greatest act of self-care. Again, I encourage you to care for your well-being as you read and know that you can always pause and return to this book when you're ready.

I also want to encourage you to be a courageous reader. You practice courage when you risk self-reflection, especially when it feels uncomfortable. Sometimes you may find yourself wondering, "Wait, am I one of the *other teachers*?" Personally, I know that this has been true for me at times in my career as an educator. I have said and done things that left my colleagues feeling disrespected and diminished. However, I also believe that we grow when we self-reflect, accept responsibility for the difficult parts of ourselves, and commit to doing better.

If you are fortunate enough not to relate to any of the difficult experiences shared in these pages, my hope is that you still gain knowledge and skills to cultivate a psychologically safe work environment for yourself and others. For those of you who experience negative dynamics at work but prefer not to acknowledge them due to an inner resolve to focus only on positive things, this book will be a hard read for you. I invite you to think as though it were a guide to organizational composting. Composting is a natural process where waste can be used to nourish healthy vegetation. Composting seems like magic, but it's nature at work. By exploring harmful workplace dynamics, we are better able to understand them and take action to transform them. This is a hard thing to do alone and easier to accomplish together. Take what you learn from this book, and start within your sphere of influence, which may be a relationship with a particular colleague or with your grade-level or department team. Begin where and when you can.

Over the past several years, I have traveled the United States facilitating professional development sessions and coaching educators on trauma-informed teaching and leading. Much of my work has focused specifically on educator well-being and resilience. Over the past several years, I've had the privilege to work with thousands of educators who devote themselves to addressing the holistic needs of their students. One thing I have come to know with certainty about educators is that we dare greatly, do hard things, and make magic happen.

As you reflect on the following stories, notice your thoughts and feelings. They are valuable sources of information that will deepen the insights and actions you take away from these pages.

JAYDA

Jayda is in her third year as a high school math teacher. She is skilled at building positive relationships with her students and engaging even the most reluctant learners. In fact, she is the only math teacher at her school who hosts after-school tutoring sessions, which are packed with students who voluntarily come for additional help and practice. Jayda puts a great deal of effort into assessing her students' learning and using that data to tailor her daily instruction. The evidence of her impact is found not only in the enthusiasm that she generates among her students but also in their performance. Most of her students exceed the standards of the state's summative math assessment.

When I asked Jayda how she felt about her successes as a teacher, her response was "exhausted." She shared that although having positive relationships with her students was a source of joy, it was also hard work. The emotional labor required to build and sustain those relationships, in addition to all the other demands of teaching, took what little energy she had left. However, for Jayda these relationships fulfilled her sense of purpose, which made the extra effort she put into them worth it. Her strongest relationships, though, were with her students, not her peers. Among her colleagues, Jayda was lonely.

Jayda wanted a greater sense of connection and camaraderie with her colleagues. She wanted someone to share ideas and strategies with when she found herself struggling with a student. Instead, she felt like she worked in a school where each classroom was its own island. At best, teachers were stretched thin, and there was no time for them to build relationships with one another. At worst, teachers were burnt out and took their frustrations out on one another through relational aggression and workplace bullying.

Jayda told me about a recent experience she had at a department meeting. She said, "I walked into the meeting, and I could hear my department chair criticizing me to another teacher. She was saying that she didn't think my instruction was rigorous enough and that I babied my students with too much hand-holding." I asked Jayda how she felt when this happened. "I was hurt," Jayda said, "but I wasn't surprised. She's a gossip and she's always finding fault with people. She has a little group of teachers who fawn over her because she's close with the principal. She and the principal have lunch together some days. And every year she hosts the holiday staff party at her house, so she has a lot of social power too."

I asked Jayda if she had any thoughts as to why she was the target of her colleague's criticism. "I've thought about that a lot because I've always been polite and professional with her," Jayda explained. "I don't know if it is because my students do so well and she's jealous. But that might not be it. I'm the only person of color in my department, and I am at least 10 years younger than everyone else. Most of our students are students of color. So, I hear from a colleague that my department chair said to the principal, 'Of course Jayda's students bond with her. She's more like them than we are.' Can you believe she said that? I give my whole heart to my students, and she chalks it up to my race and my age. That's insulting. She invalidated me and my work."

Jayda didn't feel it would be worth confronting her department chair, nor did she think the principal would listen and respond to her concerns. In fact, she feared advocating for herself would only invite retaliation and further social exclusion. Jayda felt powerless and alone. She confessed, "I'd like to at least have a friend here. Not all the teachers are like her [the department chair]. It's just that we're so busy that a lot of teachers keep to themselves. We don't get past hello or good morning."

KURT

Kurt is a social studies teacher at a suburban high school that he attended growing up. Even though it's his first year teaching, he has known several staff members for years, a few since he was a kid. Despite feeling connected to his colleagues, Kurt has had a rocky start to the beginning of his teaching career.

When I met Kurt, he was weeks behind on his pacing calendar and panicked about catching his students up. One reason he was so far behind was that he had a hard time maintaining consistent routines and behavioral expectations in his classroom. He very much wanted his students to like him, and he felt uncomfortable when he needed to redirect their behavior. He tried to leverage relationships and use humor as much as possible when responding to challenging behaviors, but students learned quickly that they could get away with a lot in his classroom. As a result, his classes felt chaotic, and he felt like a "nice guy" being taken advantage of. The classroom chaos only partially distracted him from the fact that many of his students were not making academic progress, and he had no idea how to help them.

"I feel like I'm failing my students," Kurt admitted. I could sense the deep shame he felt as he shared this with me. It's painful to hear things like this from a teacher, especially one who is only beginning his career as an educator. However, I can relate. To put it bluntly, during my first year of teaching, I was a hot mess, but with some coaching and opportunities to learn from my colleagues and my own mistakes, I improved. Still, there remains the undeniable moral trauma of working in an under-resourced field like public education and encountering a need that surpasses your capacity to respond. Sadly, I have met many new teachers who carry the shame of our broken system. They don't get support they need, they blame themselves, and they leave the field of education. We cannot carry the weight of our duty as educators alone; we are far more resilient and impactful when we work together.

I asked Kurt about the types of support he received as a new teacher in hopes that he would stop blaming himself and see that developing one's craft as an educator is a journey of progress, not perfection. Kurt's onboarding experience consisted of a half-day new teacher orientation spent reviewing the employee handbook. Then he was given the keys to his classroom, and a mug with the school's logo on it, and told to have a great year. Kurt relied on his intuition and the skills he had started to develop during the student teaching he did in graduate school. If the door to his classroom was closed, he felt some modicum of relief knowing no one else would be bothered by the mayhem in his room—at least until about a month into the school year when a fight broke out in his sixth-period class that erupted into the hallway. In the days following the incident, the principal came in to observe Kurt's classes multiple times.

I asked if the principal offered him any helpful feedback. "Not really," Kurt said. "He told me what needed to be improved, but he didn't offer any suggestions for how to go about making those changes happen." Regardless of his administrator's capacity to be of assistance, Kurt has several colleagues with years of experience who could offer their support and wisdom. I suggested that he try to connect with one of them perhaps as a mentor. "It's not like that here," he replied. "We compete with each other more than we collaborate. The principal starts off the year reminding us of the teachers whose students performed the best on last year's state tests. That pretty much sets the tone. As a teacher, you need to focus on the test scores and make sure your students do better than everybody else's."

Kurt went on to say, "We talk to each other about football or what we did on our last vacation, but we don't talk about problems we're facing as teachers. I mean we might vent about a student, but nobody is going to ask for suggestions about how to work with that kid because that makes it look like *you* are the problem, not the student." This is a common dynamic that reveals the seductive appeal that blame holds when teachers don't feel safe enough to learn. By making the student the problem, the educator alleviates their own shame or fear that they aren't a good enough teacher. The onus of responsibility for changing the situation is placed on the student. Sadly, this is a sure-fire way to ensure things will either remain the same or worsen.

Kurt explained that when he has asked his colleagues questions about ways to better support students, he hasn't received much guidance. "I get raised eyebrows or judgmental responses like "Oh so *that* is how you've been teaching it?" It's almost like they don't think I'm capable of teaching. The worst times for me are when I do something that I think is the right thing to do and get reprimanded. Like the other day, I sent a student to the office because of his behavior, and then I was told that's not how we handle things here. Well, no one told me how to handle things here; otherwise, I'd do what's expected of me."

Kurt's frustration is a classic example of an educator who works in a school where it isn't safe to learn. Asking questions, seeking help, and making mistakes are framed as deficits rather than opportunities to learn and grow. When it seems like everything that we've tried has failed to benefit a struggling student, when we've reached the limit of our compassion with a student's challenging behaviors, when we've taught it but our students didn't learn it—these are some of the many instances when we need to be able to share our frustrations and brainstorm solutions with our colleagues. Supportive work environments provide structured opportunities to ask questions, share knowledge, and offer constructive feedback and support. These schools make it safe enough for educators to learn.

JOAN

Joan has been teaching fifth grade for 20 years. She is an exceptional teacher. She is beloved by her students and many of their families. Joan has a strong connection with her grade-level team. They listen, problem-solve, and support one another. Joan feels that teaching is not simply a job, rather it is a vocation. Somehow after two decades in the profession, she continues to find delight and wonder in her work. This is not to say that she doesn't also find teaching to be exhausting, difficult, and overwhelming at times. She is, after all, a teacher and a human being.

I met Joan at a professional development workshop that I was attending as a fellow participant. We became instant friends. Her warm demeanor and enthusiasm were infectious, even to me as an adult. I had no trouble imagining her in the classroom captivating her students' attention and stoking their curiosity and excitement for learning. I caught myself resenting the fact that she wasn't leading our training because she emanated more passion for the subject than our facilitator.

After the workshop, Joan and I exchanged numbers to stay in touch. Over the next several months we texted and had a few phone calls to catch up. I continued to appreciate her uplifting spirit, and she shared that she valued my authenticity and candor. One afternoon, I got a call from her and could tell immediately from the sound of her voice that something was wrong. Her voice was shaky like she was about to cry. She said to me, "Today my principal observed my class and told me that my students are lucky to have me." I then heard the quiet hiccups of her breaking into tears.

I said, "Joan that's great news. Of course, they're lucky to have you. But what's wrong? It sounds like you're crying." She spoke between what were now full sobs, "I've had this principal for 15 years, and this is the first compliment she has given me. Fifteen years." Joan was grieving years of devoting her mind, heart, physical energy, money, and time in the hopes that her efforts would be valued not only by her students but also by the leader of her school.

My mind scrambled to make sense of the situation. Her principal must have acknowledged her impact before now. Perhaps the principal was busy supporting struggling teachers and assumed she could leave well enough alone. Or maybe the principal was frustrated because her own efforts weren't being acknowledged by her supervisors at the district office. I stopped myself before I voiced any of these unhelpful rationalizations. Instead, I listened as Joan cried.

Teaching tests our minds, bodies, and emotions every school day, and the desire to have someone acknowledge our hard work is a valid need. We invest a great deal into our students in the hopes that what we teach will benefit them now and in the future. For those of us like Joan, who bring our whole self to this profession, we are transformed and challenged by it.

Only a fellow educator can relate to the demand and depth of our profession. Educators work extremely hard to meet students' cognitive, behavioral, and social-emotional needs, and we deserve to be appropriately acknowledged, appreciated, and compensated.

TONI

Toni is the principal of a large urban school that serves students in kindergarten to eighth grade. She is a dynamic principal who works well beyond the hours of the school day to address the needs of staff, students, and families. However, she often feels like her hard work falls short of meeting their needs. She admitted, "My day gets hijacked. I've got to de-escalate a kid who tore apart a classroom; an upset parent needs to talk to me; I need to facilitate a restorative conversation about a fight that happened on the playground; some maintenance issue still hasn't been repaired even though the work order was submitted a week ago; it's one little crisis after another. By the time I sit down and look at the to-do list that I made that morning, all I can do is laugh to avoid crying."

Toni shared candidly, "It doesn't help that the district keeps introducing all these new initiatives, and none of them align with each other. So, I have to be the bad guy who gives my teachers yet another thing to do. It's easy to lose sight of our purpose because we're so busy trying to check off the boxes in order to comply with the district's agenda." I asked Toni if she had a leadership team at her school that she could turn to for support, and her response was interesting. She said, "I think my teachers want to make me happy." This made me curious, so I asked if I could sit in on a meeting with Toni and some of the teachers at her school.

Toni invited me to join a fifth grade team meeting. The purpose of the meeting was to review data from a recent literacy assessment and discuss needed instructional changes. The literacy assessment revealed that most fifth grade students were reading at a third grade level. Despite the disappointing data, the teachers remained pleasant and agreeable. When Toni broke down the data by subgroups (emerging language learners, students with individualized education programs (IEPs), etc.), the group turned ever so slightly toward blame. One teacher said she was curious if the students' parents read to them at home. Another asserted that the texts in the district's new curriculum weren't engaging. While they levied these complaints, everyone maintained smiles on their faces.

Toni asked if they had been implementing any of the strategies from the district's professional development trainings on differentiated instruction for literacy. Everyone emphatically agreed that they were each using the strategies and doing all that they could to support their students. Then the meeting ended. There was no plan made as to what to differently in light of the data but simply a shared agreement that everyone was doing the best they could despite a boring curriculum and parents who allegedly don't read to their kids.

After the meeting, I asked Toni if she felt the meeting was effective. She said, "No. Not at all. That's just the first part of the process though. In the meeting everyone plays nice. Tomorrow, they'll each try to find a time to meet with me individually, and they'll throw each under the bus. That's when I'll learn what really goes on in their classrooms when I'm not in there for observations." Toni's response reveals a school that values niceness over authenticity and impact. To be clear, when I use the word "nice," I am not referring to kindness. Instead, I am referring to a culture that avoids conflict and genuine communication in favor of superficial interactions that maintain the status quo. In schools that prioritize niceness, the needs of the students are often neglected to make the adults more comfortable.

In "nice" schools, staff avoid tough conversations about topics such as improving instruction, addressing inequities, or failing to follow through on their commitments. Staff let one another off the hook for not meeting their professional duties with the expectation that their colleagues will return the favor. As a result, the quality of instruction suffers, and the adults working in the school suffer as well. "Nice" schools are often psychologically unsafe places to work. When schools don't have structures in place that allow their staff to address problems in a productive manner, the problems fester. Educators in these schools often resort to gossip, backstabbing, scapegoating, and other forms of indirect aggression to vent their frustration. "Nice" schools can be painful places to work despite the smile on everyone's face.

COLLECTIVE EFFICACY

To meet the academic, behavioral, and social-emotional needs of students, educators must work together as a team. Having everyone on the same page allows for consistency and a systemic approach to the holistic care and education of students. Otherwise, every classroom functions in a silo with each teacher doing what they think is best. When this happens, parents are forced to gamble each year with their child's future. Will their child be lucky enough to get the teacher who is skilled at building relationships, tailoring instruction, and assessing learning? Or will their child get the teacher in the classroom next door who spends most of the day at their desk while students do busywork? This is what some refer to as *success by chance* rather than *success by design*. Success by design necessitates productive collaboration among educators that builds collective efficacy.

Collective efficacy is a belief shared among educators that when they work together as a team, they can improve student outcomes. In practice, collective efficacy is both a belief and a process of continual improvement that is guided by shared goals, sustained through teamwork, and informed by evidence of impact. John Hattie's Visible Learning research has found collective efficacy to be one of the greatest influences on student achievement. In fact, students in schools with high levels of collective efficacy often achieve 2 years' worth of academic growth in a year's worth of time. Collective efficacy has also been shown to mitigate the harmful effects of poverty on learning, making it a defining characteristic of high-performing, high-poverty schools.[1] Teams and teamwork are at the heart of collective efficacy. There can be no collective efficacy without effective collaboration. Effective collaboration is built upon trust and psychological safety.

Between 2013 and 2015, Google conducted research on the defining characteristics of high-performing teams within their company. Researchers interviewed more than 200 Google employees, studied the dynamics of more than 180 teams within the company, and analyzed more than 250 different influences on team performance. Going into the study, researchers assumed that the effectiveness of a team would be largely determined by the level of expertise of the team members. However, they were surprised to learn that a team's effectiveness is not determined by who is on the team but instead by how the members of the team interact with one another. The study's findings revealed five key characteristics of high-performing teams:

1. **Psychological Safety:** Team members trust one another enough to take risks.
2. **Dependability:** Team members can rely on one another to each do their part.
3. **Structure and Clarity:** There are clearly defined goals, roles, and responsibilities.

4. **Meaning of the Work:** Team members feel that their work is meaningful.
5. **Impact of the Work:** Team members know their work makes a difference.

Of these five factors, researchers found that psychological safety had the greatest influence on a team's effectiveness.[2] In many respects, psychological safety is the foundation upon which the other characteristics are built.

Harvard Business School professor and author Amy Edmondson defines psychological safety as "a shared belief held by members of a team that the team is safe for interpersonal risk taking."[3] In terms of school teams, this would look like colleagues who trust one another enough to take the risks that are required to grow their skills and improve student outcomes, risks like asking questions, sharing new ideas, offering support, valuing someone else's contributions, and confronting problems and challenges.

Author and CEO, Dr. Timothy R. Clark has said, "Psychological safety is a condition in which human beings feel included, safe to learn, safe to contribute and safe to challenge the status quo—all without fear of being embarrassed, marginalized, or punished in some way." Clark has defined four stages of psychological safety that reveal how psychological safety is developed and sustained in our workplaces.[4]

1. **Inclusion Safety:** Colleagues feel welcomed, included, and respected by one another.
2. **Learner Safety:** Colleagues ask questions, seek help, share feedback, and learn from mistakes.
3. **Contributor Safety:** Colleagues acknowledge and value one another's contributions.
4. **Challenger Safely:** Colleagues address challenges and problems in a productive manner.

Each of these stages builds upon the preceding one. For example, if you don't feel included at work, then you are far less likely to ask questions and seek support. Therefore, a school team's journey begins with belonging and evolves into tackling tough challenges in ways that make an impact while inspiring team members with a greater sense of confidence in their collective ability.

Let's reflect for a moment on the four vignettes that we explored earlier in this chapter. Jayda's story shows us how lonely and exhausting it is to work at a school where inclusion safety is missing. Kurt's story reveals an educator who has no experience of learner safety and finds himself feeling judged and frustrated. Joan's tears are the result of years of having an administrator who failed to cultivate a sense of contributor safety for a highly effective teacher. Finally, we learn about Toni's school, which struggles to meet the learning needs of its students because staff aren't having the growth-producing conversations that can happen only when challenger safety has been established. Each of these stories offers insight into the critical role that psychological safety plays in fostering both educator well-being and effectiveness.

In this book, we will explore each of the four stages of psychological safety as they relate to creating healthy and high-performing schools. We'll also look at factors that contribute to psychologically unsafe work environments for educators. In each section of the book, we'll use real-life case studies and research to identify what can be done to cultivate inclusion, learner, contributor, and challenger safety for you and your colleagues. Before we go any further on this journey, I invite you take a moment to reflect on your experience of psychological safety at work.

EDUCATOR PSYCHOLOGICAL SAFETY ASSESSMENT

Please read the following statements and decide how strongly you agree or disagree with each of them.

1. Staff members within my school can bring up problems, challenges, and tough issues.
2. I feel safe enough to try new strategies within my school.
3. It is difficult to ask other staff members at my school for help.
4. I feel safe expressing my ideas, questions, and concerns at work.
5. None of my colleagues would intentionally undermine my efforts.
6. At my school, my unique skills and talents are recognized, valued, and utilized.
7. My colleagues and I learn from and with one another.
8. If I make a mistake at work, it will likely be held against me.

(Continued)

(Continued)

9. If I share about a success at work, my colleagues will respond positively.
10. Colleagues within my school sometimes reject others for being different from them.

These statements are adapted from Edmondson, A. (1999). Psychological safety and learning behavior in work teams. Administrative Science Quarterly, *44(2), 350–383.*

REFLECTION QUESTIONS

1. Reflect upon the statements from the Educator Psychological Safety Assessment. What do these statements reveal about your experience of psychological safety at your school?
2. Do you relate to any of the experiences that were shared in the stories of Jayda, Kurt, Joan, and Toni? If so, how?
3. Of the four stages of psychological safety (inclusion, learner, contributor, challenger), is there one that feels especially important to you? Why or why not?
4. If a colleague had never heard of the concept of psychological safety, how would you describe it to them?

KEY TAKEAWAYS

- How educators treat one another at work influences their job satisfaction and performance.
- Collective efficacy is a belief shared among educators that they can improve student outcomes. This belief becomes a reality through productive collaboration informed by evidence of impact.
- Collective efficacy drives student achievement. Psychological safety creates the conditions for collective efficacy to be possible.

- Psychological safety describes a workplace culture in which educators feel safe enough to ask questions, express concerns, share ideas, and challenge the status quo.
- Psychological safety can be built in stages through communication and behaviors that cultivate belonging, learning, appreciation, and innovation.

A note about the tool kits: Each chapter will conclude with a tool kit comprised of practices, strategies, and tools. The tool kits are divided based on behaviors for an individual educator, a team of educators, or an administrator who is leading their whole school in becoming more psychologically safe.

PRACTICES, STRATEGIES, AND TOOLS

Individual Educator
• Be mindful of how you engage with colleagues. Begin to reflect on how your words and behaviors affect how psychologically safe your coworkers feel around you. • Notice who you talk with at work and who you do not. Reflect on any perceptions or circumstances that might shape how you choose to interact with colleagues. • Observe how your colleagues interact with one another. For now, simply notice how these interactions enhance or diminish psychological safety.
Team
• Invite each team member to share their thoughts about how psychological safety affects teamwork. • As a team, brainstorm a list of behaviors that build psychological safety among your team. Invite each team member to share one behavior that they will be intentional about doing more often. Express encouragement or gratitude any time someone on the team engages in one of these behaviors.
Administrator
• Reflect on your interactions with staff. Notice how your communication and leadership style affect the degree of psychological safety within your school. • Create a psychological safety survey using the 10 statements from the end of this chapter. Have staff complete the survey anonymously by rating their agreement with each statement on a Likert-scale ranging from *strongly disagree* to *strongly agree*. You can find a sample educator psychological safety assessment at the end of the book. You can use the results of this survey to inform a school-wide psychological safety action plan (see Chapter 8). • Learn more about collective efficacy by reading articles, research studies, or books, such as Jenni Donohoo's *Collective Efficacy: How Educators' Beliefs Impact Student Learning.*

2

BURNOUT AND PSYCHOLOGICAL SAFETY

Before we go further in our exploration of psychological safety, we need to address the elephant in the room: *burnout*. Burnout and psychological safety have an interesting relationship. When the majority of a school's staff is experiencing burnout, levels of psychological safety are typically low. Burnt-out staff are more likely to either take their stress and frustration out on their colleagues or to isolate themselves at work in the interest of self-preservation. Fortunately, when psychological safety increases in the workplace, burnout among staff decreases. By creating a psychologically safe schools, we eliminate some of the major causes of burnout for educators. Afterall, when educators feel connected, supported, valued, and inspired, they are less likely to develop burnout.

If you are reading this and suspect that you are currently experiencing burnout, don't despair. I have found that through self- and collective care, we can alleviate burnout in ways that free up more energy and nurture psychological safety. Let's explore some of the ways that can happen. First, we'll discuss the signs and symptoms of burnout; then we'll explore ways to recover and heal.

THE STAGES OF BURNOUT

Let's explore what burnout is and then ways to address it both individually and collectively. To do this, I like to use a framework developed by psychologists Herbert Freudenberger and Gail North.[1] Freudenberger and North identified 12 stages of burnout. They proposed this 12-stage model decades ago; however, authors, researchers, clinicians, and professionals from a variety of fields continue to utilize it as a framework for understanding burnout. An individual may experience some of these stages and not others. I have found that the stages often occur in a chronological progression.

Understanding these stages can help us assess the degree to which we are experiencing burnout and allows us to see that burnout isn't an all-or-nothing phenomena: There are degrees of severity. If we can catch ourselves in the earlier stages of burnout, we will have an easier time addressing it. When we understand that burnout has a trajectory, we can do something to prevent things from getting worse.

I am going to list each stage of burnout as well as its associated signs and symptoms. As you read, I invite you to reflect on how you're feeling and functioning at work. Try to reflect upon the past month at work if you can and not only how you are feeling right now. There are always really bad days or really good days that can influence our thinking in that moment. So, try to think more broadly about how you have been feeling and functioning.

STAGE 1: THE COMPULSION TO PROVE ONESELF

Most of us become educators because we want to make a difference. The first two ingredients that you need for burnout are a desire to do your job well and working in a demanding field, especially one that is under-resourced like education. As a result, the work can feel endless. We often work well beyond the hours of the school day and many of us take on, or are assigned, additional duties that are needed for our school to function adequately.

STAGE 2: WORKING HARDER

We move into Stage 2 of burnout when our to-do list becomes endless and everything begins to feel urgent. If we feel part of a team and are encouraged to practice self-care, set ambitious yet achievable goals, establish reasonable timelines, prioritize responsibilities, collaborate, delegate, and/or ask for assistance, then we are likely to avoid progressing to another stage burnout.

However, many of us work in schools that do not have these behaviors and systems in place. As a result, we push ourselves to work harder and get more done.

STAGE 3: NEGLECTING NEEDS

In Stage 3, work crowds out time for other things. We start to neglect our personal needs because we simply don't have the time or energy. The third stage of burnout typically shows up as changes in diet (either skipping meals or overindulging in food as a way to self-soothe, especially sugar and caffeine), not getting enough sleep, changing or canceling plans with family and friends, not having the time or energy to do things we enjoy, and not getting adequate movement or exercise, all due to how busy and exhausted we are from work.

STAGE 4: DISPLACEMENT OF CONFLICTS

Stage 4 is a fascinating stage of burnout because our inability or lack of opportunity to establish boundaries related to work reveals itself in the form of misplaced conflict. Rather than having tough conversations with ourselves, our supervisors, or our colleagues in which we might say things like "no," "not yet," "this is a more reasonable timeline," "for me to do that I will need this," or "can we collaborate and share the work load," we accept the additional work. As a result, we start to experience conflict in other areas of our work and home life. We may find ourselves always apologizing for being late to meetings, forgetting to return work emails, or not completing tasks on time or unable to fulfill other responsibilities at work because our plates are so full.

We may also experience what I call "the pressure-cooker effect," which is when we bottle up all the stress we experience during the workday and end up unleashing it on someone outside of work. For example, we make it through the school day doing our best to stay calm and pleasant. But when we get home, with the slightest provocation from another person, we snap, and that individual gets the full brunt of our day. When I've experienced this, the worst part is how much I feel hijacked by the stress. As the argument is happening, I can tell that this person doesn't deserve the way I am treating them, and yet I can't stop myself. It's like I'm looking for a conflict to discharge some of the stress that got bottled up inside me during work. If you can relate to this, don't worry; we will explore ways to prevent this from happening later in the chapter.

STAGE 5: REVISION OF VALUES

Stage 5 was once described as the point at which the "personal horizon becomes narrow." This stage is dangerous to relationships both personal and professional. The impact of chronic stress on our brains and nervous systems, coupled with the neglect of our personal needs from Stage 3, leads to a distorted sense of time and values. We feel rushed to get things done, and we risk sacrificing relationships for our professional agenda. This can look like the educator who stops collaborating with their team because the common planning time feels inefficient: Rather than raising a concern about restructuring planning so that it is more effective, the educator simply gives up on the process and loses faith in their colleagues. One of the earliest warning signs of Stage 5 is a change in the style and tone of our communication. For myself, I can tell I am in Stage 5 when I begin to talk to colleagues in ways that are blunt, calculated, and/or insensitive because I am thinking only about what I need to get accomplished while forgetting about the person I am communicating with.

This can also look like a school leader who feels so much pressure from district administrators that they railroad their staff—ignoring their input, concerns, and ideas—and resort to fear-based tactics (threats of negative evaluations, excessive criticism, etc.) to ensure compliance. Personal relationships during this stage can be damaged at times beyond repair. This stage plants the seeds that can eventually blossom into parent-child conflict, divorce, and friendships ending because those we care about feel that we have chosen our job over them.

STAGE 6: DENIAL OF EMERGING PROBLEMS

The more burnt-out we feel, the less likely we are to recognize burnout. You might ask someone in Stage 6, "Are you feeling burnt-out at work?" And you might get a response like, "No I'm not burnt-out. I just have to work with incompetent adults and teach disrespectful children." In this stage of burnout, our thinking gets distorted. We often fall under the spell of a stress-induced negativity bias that leads to us blaming others or ourselves for the stress we are facing at work. We lose sight of the fact that we may need to take responsibility for our own well-being and do something to manage our symptoms of burnout.

The tricky part is that our ability to take action, whether it is through self-care or making changes in our workplace, can vary greatly upon the level of privilege and power we have at work as well as the degree of psychological safety in our workplace. If you work in a school where you feel heard and have some say in decision-making, then you have a better opportunity to improve your situation. However, if you work in a deeply hierarchical workplace rife with power differentials and inequitable interpersonal dynamics, then it will be much harder, if not impossible, to shift things at work.

STAGE 7: WITHDRAWAL

In Stage 7, we withdraw from relationships that once felt important. We skip our close friend's birthday party because we don't have the energy. We feel as though our spouse, children, and loved ones are more of a burden then a source of joy and connection. Perhaps we once attended baby showers, weddings, and special events with our colleagues, and now we find ourselves looking for ways to get out of having to attend these events. We might also feel incredibly guilty for feeling and behaving this way.

We may have started some of these withdrawal behaviors in one of the earlier stages of burnout, but now they become more pronounced, and the impact on our relationships is greater. We truly start to feel disconnected from some of the people in our lives. The tensions run deeper, the arguments start easily, and we find ourselves feeling resentful, alone, and at times flooded with too many emotions or completely numb.

This is a stage of burnout when we become the most vulnerable to addictive and compulsive behaviors to alleviate stress and pain. The glass of wine turns into a bottle. The scoop of ice cream turns into finishing off the entire pint. If these coping behaviors persist, they can develop into addictions. Some educators suffer in silence struggling with compulsive behaviors related to eating, gambling, screen time, exercise, shopping, hoarding, and so on. Sometimes the addiction becomes work, which can be a dangerous trap when our supervisors and colleagues praise us for working an excessive and unhealthy amount. As one educator said to me, "Ricky, I work all weekend because school is the only place where I still feel a sense of control. My physical health, my finances, my marriage—they're all a mess, and I don't want to face them. At least at school I know that I'm good at what I do." This is a trap and clear sign of Stage 7.

STAGE 8: OBVIOUS BEHAVIORAL CHANGES

Many educators in Stage 8 become cynical and apathetic and begin to shirk responsibilities, cut corners, and avoid accountability. Colleagues may note that someone who was once a team player has retreated into the background. They are more argumentative and easily frustrated. Relationships with coworkers and students can become increasingly negative. Not all of us experience Stage 8 in terms of our work performance. For many of us, our behavior change is most obvious to the people we share our more personal lives with: the friend who says, "You don't show up for me any more like you used to" or the romantic partner who says, "You ought to quit your job; you're always miserable." Statements like these are often painful to hear. They don't offer much in terms of solutions, but they point out that our unhealthy work life has done harm to our relationships.

Another common characteristic of Stage 8 is a fear and resentment of feedback even if it is constructive. This fear of feedback makes sense. In Stage 8, we feel overwhelmed and stretched too thin. We don't have the mental, emotional, or physical bandwidth to do more, yet we continue to push ourselves. Any type of feedback that invites us to grow professionally can feel like an attack, like we are being targeted and told to do even more and that our efforts are still not enough even though we feel overwhelmed, exhausted, and pushed past our limits.

STAGE 9: DEPERSONALIZATION

Depersonalization can show up in a variety of ways. We can begin to feel as though our needs are not valid. We get so accustomed to neglecting our personal needs, which started in Stage 3, that we forget that our needs even deserve to be fulfilled. Our focus is placed entirely upon productivity. Some try to justify this stage of burnout by living life at extremes, the "work hard play hard" maxim that can lead to folks feeling deeply depleted but too busy to notice.

Depersonalization can also extend to others. This is common in health care when patients are no longer seen as people and receive a diminished quality of attention, empathy, and care. However, this happens for educators as well. We risk losing sight of our students, focusing exclusively on test scores, pacing calendars, and content rather than acknowledging and engaging our students' unique strengths, talents, identities, and needs. During Stage 9, some of us may also engage in presenteeism: We show up for work physically but are checked out mentally and emotionally. This is a dangerous place for an educator to be because we lose connection to both the positive difference we make and the harm we might cause by not being self-aware.

STAGE 10: INNER EMPTINESS

We get to the end of the workday, and all we can think about is what we messed up, didn't get done, or have to do tomorrow. We don't notice the student who we made smile when we greeted them or the progress one of our students made in their learning. In Stage 10, we may feel numb, inadequate, exhausted, anxious, and even panicked. We are saturated with stress hormones that make it hard to rest and recover. Instead, we feel full of adrenaline or "tired and wired." We can start to dread work. Some of us may even experience panic attacks and severe anxiety. As soon as someone even mentions the topic of work, our blood pressures rises, or we feel a heavy weight descend upon us.

STAGE 11: DEPRESSION

Stage 11 is characterized by persistent feelings of hopelessness and despair. It is no surprise that we find ourselves feeling depressed. We have given our all, and more is still needed. The depression can be so severe that we may begin to wish harm upon ourselves or others. Many educators in Stage 11 experience suicidal thoughts and impulses. If we struggle with addiction, those behaviors may become unmanageable to the point of threatening our life. We cannot go on like this.

STAGE 12: BURNOUT SYNDROME

We find ourselves in the emergency room with symptoms of a heart attack. We get medical results that are concerning. Our mental health has depleted to the extent that medication and therapies are now gravely needed. Burnout syndrome is a mental, emotional, and physical reality characterized by depression, anxiety, irritability, and significant fluctuations in mood, and it can manifest in a variety of physical ailments including but not limited to headaches, digestive problems, heart palpations, shortness of breath, dizziness, high blood pressure, and so on.

REFLECTION QUESTIONS

1. Are you currently experiencing any of these stages of burnout? If so, which ones?
2. Over the course of your career in education, have there been times when your experience of burnout was more severe than other times? What contributed to this?

Stages of Burnout

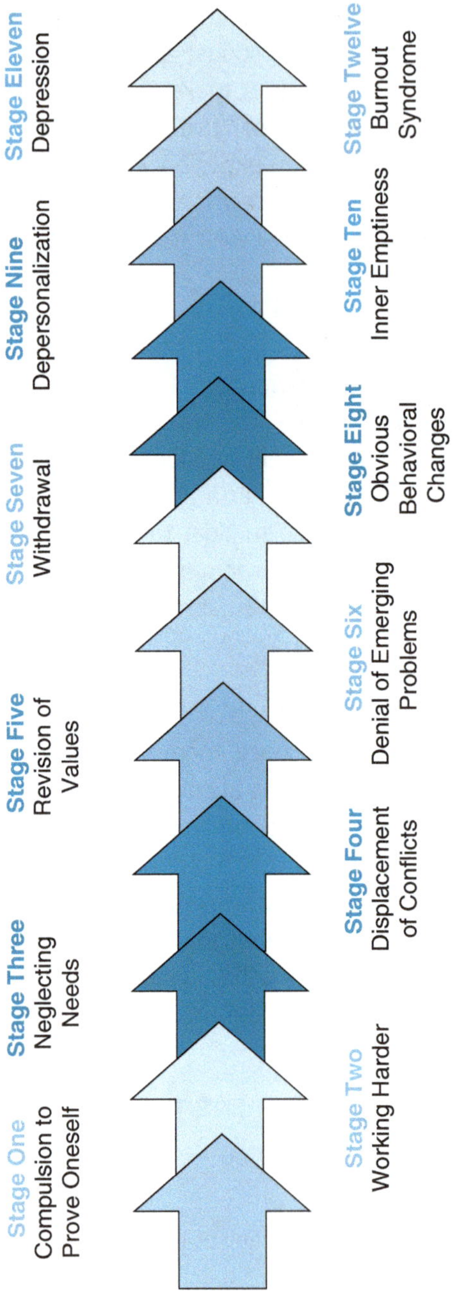

Stage One Compulsion to Prove Oneself

Stage Two Working Harder

Stage Three Neglecting Needs

Stage Four Displacement of Conflicts

Stage Five Revision of Values

Stage Six Denial of Emerging Problems

Stage Seven Withdrawal

Stage Eight Obvious Behavioral Changes

Stage Nine Depersonalization

Stage Ten Inner Emptiness

Stage Eleven Depression

Stage Twelve Burnout Syndrome

SPEAKING TRUTH TO BURNOUT

BURNING THE CANDLE AT BOTH ENDS: HIGHLY EFFECTIVE AND BURNT-OUT

Before moving forward, I want to dismantle a few stereotypes and misconceptions of burnout. The first stereotype is that all burnt-out teachers are apathetic and bad at their jobs. Although many do become increasingly apathetic and negative (especially as they move into the more advanced stages of burnout), research shows that many educators are both highly effective at their jobs and burnt-out. These are the educators who "burn the candle at both ends." They may be exceptional teachers, caring colleagues, and a devoted spouse, parent, and friend and find that they have no space in their life for their own needs. I find that it is actually much harder for these educators to recognize their level of burnout and take action to address it. They have a harder time recognizing it perhaps because they are both busy and passionate about their job. They may have a hard time taking action to address it because to do so would require a willingness to put up boundaries, say no, and even be the "good enough" educator at times.

BURNOUT IS NOT PERMANENT

Another common misconception about burnout is that it is permanent. When I started teaching, colleagues would say things like, "Ricky, you have to retire before you get burnt-out," as though burnout was a destination that you arrived at and never left. To be honest, this made sense to me as a new teacher. Some of my colleagues showed up physically for work, but they were checked out mentally and emotionally. They gave their students busywork and hardly engaged with them. I also thought about teachers I had growing up who seemed indifferent toward me and my classmates. At the surface level, it seemed like burnout was a stage you reached in your career where you remained, counting the days until retirement. In reality, burnout is not permanent. We can move into and out of the stages of burnout at different points in our career, even at different points in the same school year. In fact, the more aware we are of our level of burnout, the more likely we can alleviate and even prevent it.

BURNOUT IS NOT A PERSONAL FAILURE

Many of us feel guilty for experiencing burnout, as though we shouldn't feel this way, when in fact, I don't know how you could not experience burnout at some point in your career as an educator. We work within an under-resourced system in which we encounter a need that surpasses our capacity to respond. We take on the role of teacher, therapist, nurse, parent, and so many other roles to fill the gaps that many of our students have in their lives. We work in a system with an endless amount of new initiatives that are rarely, if ever, aligned and integrated into a holistic approach. We are stretched far too thin and rarely have the time or structures in place to meaningfully assess our impact and make improvements. All of this is the perfect recipe for burnout, which makes it not a personal failure but a systemic outcome. We work in a system that is built to burn us out. However, it does not have to be this way.

REFLECTION QUESTIONS

1. You can be highly effective and burnt out. Burnout is not permanent. Burnout is not a personal failure. Which one of these three statements resonates with you the most? Why?
2. Has there been a time when you were experiencing burnout and you did something that helped to alleviate it?

SELF-CARE IS ESSENTIAL

Self-care is essential for preventing and alleviating burnout. However, there are common misconceptions that can impede our ability to practice self-care in ways that genuinely feel nurturing and supportive. For example, many of us have been taught that self-care is about setting ambitious fitness or personal growth goals and working toward them. This approach has us treat self-care like a to-do list. I will go to the gym, walk at least 10,000 steps, drink at least 64 ounces of water, meditate for 30 minutes, do 10 minutes of yoga in the morning, journal before bed, and so on. When we approach self-care in this way, we run the risk of our self-care plan becoming our self-criticism plan if we don't accomplish everything on the list and fall short of our own expectations.

We practice true self-care when we recognize and respond to our needs with compassion, love, and respect. This approach to self-care invites you to focus more on the relationship you have with yourself rather than a to-do list. For example, maybe you had a horrible night's sleep, and going to the gym would leave you feeling depleted. Perhaps a healthier and more compassionate choice would be to practice gentle yoga or take a nap. After all, rest is one of the most important, yet often undervalued, forms of self-care. When it comes to maintaining healthy habits, it is best to hold tight gently. Allow yourself grace and flexibility for times when you need to modify your habits or practice other forms of self-care to meet your needs.

Let's explore ways that we can establish healthy routines while also honoring our day-to-day needs.

CREATE ELASTIC HABITS

In Stephen Guise's book *Elastic Habits: How to Create Smarter Habits That Adapt to Your Day,* he presents an approach to maintaining habits by creating three levels of intensity and success: mini, plus, and elite.[2] For example, if you have a goal to meditate for 30 minutes a day, this would be considered the plus version of your habit. Let's say that on days when you are too busy or tired, 30 minutes is not feasible. On these days, you will meditate for 3 minutes, and this is your mini version. On days when you have more time to devote to your meditation practice, you will meditate for 45 minutes, and this is the elite version of your habit. Stephen Guise has also recommended tracking your mini, plus, and elite "wins" on an app or calendar to motive yourself.

I have found this approach helpful because it saves me from the all-or-nothing approach to self-care, where I maintain healthy routines for a period of time and then get derailed by something in life (e.g., a big work project, the holidays, etc.), and I abandon my well-being. By having a mini, plus, and elite version, my habits are more flexible and resilient. Even when life is hectic, I can take some small action to support my well-being.

PRACTICE BITE-SIZE SELF-CARE DURING THE SCHOOL DAY

Stress in the classroom is contagious. In one study researchers evaluated teachers to assess their level of burnout. Researchers then got permission from students and parents to take saliva samples from students during the school day. They assessed the saliva samples for cortisol, a stress hormone, and discovered that when students entered the classrooms of highly burnt-out teachers, the level of cortisol in the students' bodies significantly increased. Over the course of the school year, students in the classrooms of highly burnt-out teachers were more likely to develop symptoms of anxiety and engage in more challenging behaviors.

A classroom full of anxious and defiant students naturally increases the stress of a highly burnt-out teacher, creating a self-reinforcing loop. As educators, the only way to disrupt this cycle is to practice bite-size acts of self-care during the workday. When we lower our stress levels, we are better able to support our students. Identify three to five simple things you can do during the school day to alleviate stress in healthy ways. Educators have shared with me a variety of strategies including talking with a colleague, listening to music, finding a private moment to pray or meditate, stepping outside when the weather is nice, doing something kind for someone, expressing gratitude in some small way, and so on.

CREATE A SELF-CARE FIRST-AID PLAN

A self-care first-aid plan is comprised of things you can do to care for yourself on your toughest days. Your self-care first-aid plan may include prayer, mindfulness practices, calling a trusted friend, therapy, comforting your body, finding time to feel your feelings, journaling, saying kind things to yourself, and so on. Think of it as treating yourself with the love and respect you would extend to a friend who is having a hard time.

Don't beat yourself up when life beats you down. If you struggle with negative self-talk and unhealthy coping behaviors, it can be helpful to write down your self-care first-aid plan and keep it somewhere that is easily accessible to you. When faced with significant stress, sometimes our brains need to be reminded of healthier ways to cope.

ESTABLISH HEALTHY BOUNDARIES

Boundaries are not simply a matter of saying yes or no. They show up in a variety of ways, and some boundaries are more malleable than others. Boundaries can look like asking for what you need, developing realistic goals and timelines, prioritizing certain aspects of your work, collaborating, delegating, or saying no. A boundary can also be as simple as deciding on a time each day when you will stop working and no longer check work-related emails. The key to establishing better boundaries is clear communication and a willingness to uphold boundaries once they've been established.

Psychologist Harriet Lerner, in her classic book *The Dance of Anger*, discusses the countermoves that people make to challenge a boundary once it is asserted.[3] Countermoves can look like the child who throws a tantrum when told no or the administrator who temporarily punishes us with the silent treatment because we told them we won't chair another committee. Countermoves are common because we are changing the established dynamic of the relationship, and change can upset people. Boundaries can be especially difficult to negotiate and maintain when there is a power differential between the parties involved (e.g., a teacher and principal, etc.). Prior to negotiating a boundary, it can be helpful to consider the risk that a potential countermove poses to your personal and professional well-being. You may decide that asserting a particular boundary is not worth the negative response you might encounter. Conversely, you might decide that a potential countermove will be a minor discomfort in establishing a boundary that is essential for you to sustain yourself in your profession. Fortunately, many countermoves can be resolved with time and communication.

Sometimes the countermove comes from us. We are the ones who erode our own boundaries. For example, I am addicted to yes. I will say yes to things even when my plate is full, especially if you convince me that it would help someone else. The trouble is that when I say no, I often feel guilty. As a result, I have had times when I have relinquished my own boundary, gone back, and said I can do it after all. If you can relate to this, then I invite you to sit with the discomfort that comes up when you say no or advocate for your needs. The discomfort is temporary; what you can't get back is the time and energy you will lose if you abandon your boundaries and yourself.

Without boundaries to protect our time and energy, maintaining healthy habits becomes nearly impossible. Having said that, practicing self-care, especially when it comes to communicating and maintaining boundaries, can be confusing and messy at times. Give yourself the grace to make mistakes and learn as you grow. Self-care is a journey of progress, not perfection. My hope is that you discover new ways to care for yourself that you genuinely enjoy.

REFLECTION QUESTIONS

1. Was there anything from our exploration of self-care that shifted, confirmed, or inspired your thinking?
2. What is one boundary that you can realistically establish and maintain to protect your time, energy, and well-being? How will you communicate this boundary to others? How will you address any potential countermoves?
3. Create an elastic habit. What is one health-promoting habit that you would like to engage in? What is a mini, plus, and elite version of that habit that would make it more feasible? How will you track and celebrate your progress?

HURTING TO HEALING TO HELPING

I have heard countless stories about the challenges that educators face in their schools. The stories of trauma experienced by educators and students weigh heaviest on my heart. Thankfully, I continue to encounter a growing number of schools that are committed to addressing the harmful effects of adverse childhood experiences (ACEs) and trauma among their students.

However, I often find that little attention is paid to the forms of trauma that many educators experience. When these forms of trauma are ignored, educators suffer in silence, and many leave the field of education. As a result, students lose out on the powerful impact these individuals could have made in their lives. A trauma-informed approach to education is critical for the well-being of both students *and* educators.

Although it is impossible to list all the forms of trauma that can affect educators in our work, I propose four broad categories, or domains, to help us identify and distinguish forms of trauma and their impact on educators. I also want to be clear about my use of the word "trauma" so that we can share a common understanding of the term. When I refer to trauma, I am referring to "an event, or series of events, or set of circumstances that is experienced by an individual as physically or emotionally harmful or threatening and has lasting adverse effects on the individual's functioning and physical, social, emotional, or spiritual well-being."[4] I have found that the forms of trauma experienced by educators often fall within the following domains:

Secondary Trauma: Secondary trauma refers to forms of trauma that occur to individuals who the educator knows and cares about, such as students, families, colleagues, and so on. As educators, the more we care, the harder this job is. When we care deeply about our students and school community, the hardships that they encounter can weigh heavily on our hearts. Secondary trauma can contribute to compassion fatigue and secondary traumatic stress among educators.

Work-Related Primary Trauma: Unlike secondary trauma, which occurs to someone else, primary trauma refers to forms of trauma that affect the individual directly. Sadly, some educators experience forms of primary trauma at work, including but not limited to school shootings, tragic accidents, physical assault by students, chronic workplace bullying, harassment, discrimination, and so on. Primary trauma can contribute to mental and physical health challenges, including posttraumatic stress.

Personal Primary Trauma: I use the phrase "personal primary trauma" to broadly refer to an educator's experiences of primary trauma and ACEs that have occurred within the educator's personal life and may affect their ability to work. When educators do not have access to care or do not seek care (e.g., therapy, social support, self-care practices, etc.) to recover and heal from their own experiences of trauma and ACEs, these experiences have the potential to hinder their ability to support students and work with colleagues.

Moral Trauma: Educators work in a highly demanding, under-resourced field. Many educators encounter needs that surpass their capacity to respond. Moral trauma sets in when an educator is continually exposed to circumstances in which students, families, and colleagues do not receive the support and resources that they need, and the educator is forced to act in ways that fail to provide students with the care that they deserve. I have found that moral trauma can contribute to low morale, burnout, and staff turnover within schools.

These four domains of trauma are by no means a complete list of all the forms of trauma that educators may experience. To address the trauma that many of us endure, we must engage in self-care, collective care, and systemic change. A trauma-informed approach to education involves implementing practices and systems within schools to recognize and respond to trauma while increasing access to protective factors, resources, and care that support the well-being of students, families, and staff. This journey begins by taking action to establish physical and psychological safety within schools.

If you are an educator who is suffering from exposure to trauma and/or ACEs, know that you are not alone. I encourage you to seek therapeutic care and social support. There are a growing number of trauma-informed therapists who can offer assistance and guidance. Cognitive behavioral therapy, eye movement desensitization and reprocessing (EMDR), and somatic therapy are among the many therapeutic modalities that have been shown to alleviate symptoms of anxiety, depression, and posttraumatic stress. When therapeutic care is coupled with healthy habits to care for the body, we can heal the whole self.

There is also a growing body of literature on recovering from trauma and healing symptoms of posttraumatic stress. Pete Walker's book *Complex PTSD: From Surviving to Thriving* is a personal favorite that helped me tremendously in my healing journey.[5] Complex posttraumatic stress disorder (CPTSD) is common among individuals who experienced verbal, physical, sexual, and/or emotional abuse growing up. CPTSD is fundamentally a struggle with emotional and physiological dysregulation that leaves many adults living in persistent states of fight, flight, freeze, or fawn. They find themselves reenacting behaviors that they used to survive their childhoods, including people pleasing, caretaking, dissociating, numbing, and so on. Fortunately, survivors of childhood trauma can recover from CPTSD and find freedom from the shame, pain, and abandonment that are carryovers from their childhoods. In his book, Pete Walker presents insights and practices that aid the healing process. For those looking to better understand trauma and healing, please see the list of additional titles in the back of this book.

Survivors of ACEs and trauma are especially vulnerable to addiction. Many of us turn to compulsive behaviors and/or substances to numb our pain. If you are struggling with addiction, there are therapists, treatment centers, and 12-step recovery fellowships where you will be welcomed and supported in coming home to yourself in healthy ways.

Healing is possible. I know it to be true for myself and countless others. You are worthy of care and well-being.

REFLECTION QUESTIONS

1. Where do you experience care and connection? Make a list of these sources of support and connection (e.g., friends, family, colleagues, spirituality, animals, nature, etc.).
2. If you have experienced ACEs and/or trauma, what is one thing you can do to support your own healing?

COLLECTIVE CARE IS NECESSARY

We discussed the stages of burnout as they relate to the individual; however, many of us work in schools where most educators are experiencing burnout, and it affects the entire school culture. In schools that suffer from collective burnout, you may have a staff member who is reluctant to try new things and looks for new initiatives to fail. The negativity bias that is associated with chronic stress sets in among the staff, and they seem to notice only shortcomings, failings, and barriers to success. Think of how many new programs, initiatives, and curriculums fail because staff are too burnt-out to implement them. Some of these initiatives may have great merit, but the staff is too fatigued to fully engage with them.

A burnt-out staff is also one in which many of its members engage in presenteeism. They show up physically work, but they are mentally and emotionally disengaged. I can relate to this experience. I have had times where it felt like it was me versus my students. I needed to survive the workday. This can be common every once in a while and is still a signal that self-care is needed. However, when it starts to feel like a daily reality, and it spreads among a staff, then you have a significant barrier to efficacy. I often see evidence of this in staff meetings during which educators are checking their phones or are on their laptops shopping on Amazon or planning their next vacation rather than participating in the discussion at hand.

When burnout is endemic within a school, it contributes to inequitable collaboration among staff. This can look like staff who don't even bother to share ideas because they feel that the effort is futile and they won't be heard. Instead, others may speak over or on behalf of their colleagues without checking in. Some administrators can find themselves burnt out and railroading staff with their agendas because they feel too busy and exhausted to seek input or build consensus. Burnout can also increase the frequency and intensity of workplace bullying behaviors as staff take their frustrations out on one another. Last, burnout can contribute to chronic absenteeism among staff and staff turnover.

Time and again I have said that self-care is essential but not enough. We also need collective care. We practice collective care by developing, implementing, and sustaining school-wide practices that support educator well-being and foster psychologically safe work environments. In my work with educators across the United States, I feel confident in saying that there is no single solution or set of practices that can be applied to every school. Instead, we must build those practices from the ground up, beginning with assessing and responding to the resiliency needs of the staff. In the coming chapters, we will explore ways to develop collective care within a school in ways that foster psychological safety.

EDUCATOR RESILIENCY NEEDS ASSESSMENT

This brief anonymous survey can be administered to school staff to gather input on ways to meet their workplace resiliency needs. A school leadership team can use the survey's responses to inform the development and implementation of school-wide collective care practices.

1. What can we do as a staff to feel more **connected?** *How can we build and maintain positive relationships among staff?*
2. What can we do as a staff to feel more **supported?** *How can we address problems and challenges together?*
3. What can we do as a staff to feel more **valued?** *How can we encourage self-care and acknowledge one another's contributions at work?*
4. What can we do as a staff to feel more **inspired?** *How can we celebrate our impact while we continually improve?*

REFLECTION QUESTIONS

1. Take the Professional Quality of Life Scale (ProQOL). The ProQOL is a free, research-based tool that assesses burnout, secondary trauma, and compassion satisfaction. You can find the ProQOL measure online at www.proqol.org. What did you learn from your results?
2. What are three to five simple things you can do during the school day to alleviate stress in healthy ways?
3. What practices are part of your self-care first-aid plan for challenging days?

KEY TAKEAWAYS

- Being aware of the signs and symptoms of burnout helps us care and advocate for ourselves.
- Burnout is not permanent. Burnout is not a personal failure. You can be highly effective and burnt-out.
- We can practice self-care by recognizing and responding to our needs with compassion, love, and respect.
- Boundaries are an essential component of self-care. Boundaries require communication and a willingness to upheld them despite countermoves.
- Educators can experience forms of trauma including secondary trauma, work-related primary trauma, personal primary trauma, and moral trauma. Trauma-informed care can support healing.
- Self-care and collective care are necessary to support educator well-being, resilience, and efficacy. Collective care involves the implementation of school-wide practices that address the needs of educators.

PRACTICES, STRATEGIES, AND TOOLS

Individual Educator
• Be mindful of signs and symptoms of burnout. Awareness is the first step in preventing burnout from getting worse. • Practice self-care during the school day and outside of work. • Establish and maintain reasonable boundaries. This process may also involve advocating for your needs and responding to countermoves. • Offer yourself grace and self-compassion. Seek support when needed. • Have fun and rest. Play and rest are important acts of self-care.
Team
• Assess your individual levels of burnout using a tool such as the ProQOL. • Share self-care strategies with one another. • Find ways to support one another, especially during particularly stressful times of the school year. • Celebrate accomplishments and find things to laugh about. These are two simple ways to reduce stress and boost resilience as a team.
Administrator
• Provide professional development to all staff about the signs and symptoms of burnout including tools to assess it (e.g., the ProQOL) and self-care strategies to mitigate it. • Administer the Educator Resiliency Needs Assessment. Work with your leadership team to develop and implement school-wide collective care practices. • Express appreciation and build relationships. Connection and gratitude are powerful buffers against work-related stress.

3

TRUST AND FEAR

Psychological safety reduces fear. Self-help author and teacher Louise Hay spoke about fear as the absence of trust.[1] We feel afraid when we can't trust ourselves, trust one another, or trust life. In schools that lack psychological safety, educators encounter significant interpersonal risks that evoke fear, compromise their well-being, and inhibit effective collaboration. These interpersonal risks can range from the risk of being viewed as incompetent to being subjected to bullying and rejection at work. We establish psychological safety in our schools through communication and behaviors that reduce interpersonal risk and build trust.

Each stage of psychological safety reduces interpersonal risks and fears through words and actions that build dimensions of trust. Inclusion safety reduces the fear of being bullied and rejected by colleagues by building the trust through authentic belonging. Learner safety reduces the fear that our ideas, questions, and mistakes will be ridiculed and held against us by building trust through shared learning. Contributor safety reduces the fear that our skills, talents, and efforts will be criticized, undervalued, and exploited by building trust through mutual appreciation, shared responsibility, and an equitable distribution of work. Challenger safety reduces the fear of personal attacks and divisive conflict by building trust through structured collaboration, healthy communication, and supportive accountability. In subsequent chapters, we will explore each stage of psychological safety in greater depth. For now, it is important to understand that each of us influences the stages of psychological safety within our schools. Our interactions with fellow educators have the power to build trust and safety or cause hurt and evoke fear.

The four stages of psychological safety (inclusion, learner, contributor, challenger) build upon one another while remaining interconnected and mutually reinforcing. Some behaviors and workplace practices influence multiple stages of psychological safety. For example, later in the book, we will explore ways that Nonviolent Communication (NVC) can strengthen both inclusion and challenger safety by enabling staff members to build positive relationships across dimensions of difference (e.g., age, race, ethnicity, gender, etc.) while also facilitating conflict resolution. However, there is no single factor that has a greater influence on all stages of psychological safety than a school administrator's leadership style.

An administrator's leadership style has a significant influence on the degree of psychological safety within a school, however, it is not the sole influence. A school develops and sustains a psychologically safe workplace culture through the combined efforts of the staff and administration. However, an administrator's leadership style can significantly strengthen or diminish the psychological safety experienced by staff. In this chapter, we will explore the story of April, an educator whose professional journey exposed her to multiple leadership styles, each having a unique influence on the psychological safety and collective efficacy within their schools.

DIVING INTO THE SHARK TANK

I met April at a national education conference where I was presenting a session on educator well-being. During the session, I mentioned that I was writing a book about psychological safety in schools. When the session was over, April came up to me and said, "I have a story for your book," and asked if we could schedule a time to talk. Like many educators whose stories are included in this book, April wanted to share her experiences to help others avoid, or liberate themselves from, similarly painful circumstances. She also wanted victims of workplace bullying and harassment to know that they are not alone, they should not blame themselves for the hurtful actions of others, and most importantly, they deserve to be treated better.

April's journey first takes us into the "shark tank," a psychologically unsafe school governed by fear, resentment, and bullying. There are themes in April's story, which I will point out along the way, that came up again and again in my interviews with educators about their experiences working in similarly hostile environments. Thankfully, April's story is also the story of an educator who reclaims her power and finds a psychologically safe school to work in, one that supports and values her. As we are about to see, April's journey offers valuable insights into the essential role that psychological safety plays in creating schools that foster well-being, efficacy, and achievement for educators and students.

When April and I sat down for our first conversation, she was in her ninth year as a teacher. She had been teaching at her current school for 4 years. Prior to that, she taught in a school in the neighboring district. As she put it, she "escaped" from her previous school after enduring "5 years of abuse." I could hear the pain in her voice when she said this. I thought about the educators I have spoken to who are still suffering through toxic work environments because of a love for their students. I also thought about the individuals I've met who have left the teaching profession entirely because they couldn't find a way to sustain themselves within a system built to burn them out. I was immediately thankful April had chosen to not give up on herself and not give up on teaching.

Like many educators, April entered the profession with a wholehearted love for children and a desire to make a difference. Since her childhood, April had wanted to be a teacher. Her mother was a middle school language arts teacher, and even though most other teachers' kids spent the last week of summer break begrudgingly helping their parents set up classrooms, April loved helping her mom prepare for each new school year.

April told me that although her mother had a significant influence on her future aspirations, it was another teacher who cemented April's desire to teach elementary school. April's first grade teacher, Mrs. Broadway, made learning feel like an adventure. April told me about the time Mrs. Broadway transformed her classroom into an enchanted garden filled with plants. Gentle rain sounds played from a set of speakers hidden from view behind a fern, while she read to her students about the life cycle of the butterfly. The care, dynamism, and joy that Mrs. Broadway brought to teaching, along with the example of her mother, inspired April to follow in their footsteps as an educator.

Shortly after completing her teaching degree, April was thrilled to be offered a position as a first grade teacher. April's soon-to-be new school was also chronically low-performing with most students never learning to read at grade level. The school's suspension rates and crisis team calls surpassed other schools in the district. Although student outcomes like this might feel daunting, or even demoralizing, to many educators, April viewed them as an opportunity to make a difference. "I felt blessed," April said. "I was going to be the one to teach my students how to read, to equip them with skills that would benefit them for the rest of their lives. That's why I became a teacher because I love kids and I want the best for them." She said this with tears in her eyes and a conviction that rang true 9 years into the profession.

"When I heard other people in the district say that my school was challenging to work in," April went on, "initially I assumed they were referring to the behavior of the students. I later realized they were talking about the behavior of the staff." April explained that in retrospect there were "red flags" at her school that she wished she had paid more attention to because doing so could have saved her a lot of self-blame and inspired her to seek out a psychologically safer school sooner.

The first red flag was the lack of onboarding and support she received as a new teacher. No one welcomed her to the school community, introduced her to colleagues, offered to mentor her, or even showed her where to find the paper for the copy machine. Instead, she was left to fend for herself. When she needed advice about instruction or responding to students' behavioral needs, April found support in online teacher communities, friends who were educators at other schools, and phone calls to her mom.

April shared, "During lunch, the teachers who had been working at the school for a while would all sit together. They never invited any of the newer teachers to join them, even if there were empty seats at their tables." April explained that the newer teachers, including her, typically ate lunch alone in their classrooms. April recalled being in the staff lunchroom one day, waiting for another new teacher to finish using the microwave so that she could warm up her lunch.

"The microwave dings," April explained. "This teacher gets her food and leaves the lunchroom. The door hadn't even closed behind her, and I hear a couple teachers at one of the tables making jokes about what that teacher was wearing. That moment, I was like they are not going to do that to me. From then on, I ate lunch in the staff lunchroom. I sat alone for almost 2 months until one of them finally asked if I wanted to join her table. I passed on the offer. I had made my point. I wasn't going to be humiliated or intimidated by them."

I have heard similar stories from other educators in psychologically unsafe schools about their experiences as new staff members, experiences that range from exclusion to being the target of outright hostility. New teachers shared stories with me about being ridiculed, belittled, and scrutinized by colleagues, as though they were being tested to see if they had the wherewithal to endure their new school. Some of these stories sounded more like hazing than new teacher orientation. They knew they had passed the test, and earned membership to the group, only when they were finally invited to an outside-of-work social event, included in the gossip, let in on shared secrets, or were the audience for a joke rather than the butt of it.

Some educators shared that they bypassed these "tests" because they joined already established cliques in their school based on their race, socioeconomic status, religion, or age. As one teacher said to me, "At my school's staff meetings, all the Jamaican teachers sit together, all the Latino teachers sit together, and all the white teachers sit together. That's just how it is. You find your group, and you stay in it. And, if you don't fit in to one of those groups, then you're on your own." A diverse staff does not imply an inclusive workplace. Rigidly defined cliques, social hierarchies, and high turnover among staff are all indicators of a lack of psychological safety. The first stage of psychological safety is inclusion, which is defined by a felt sense of authentic belonging among staff. Authentic belonging in the workplace is an ongoing practice of communication, consideration, and collaboration across personal identities and professional roles.

Schools with low levels of psychological safety tend be lonely places to work. New staff are often set up to fail because these schools lack sufficient onboarding and mentoring supports. These schools also fail to implement practices to foster positive relationships among all staff (e.g., communication agreements, staff celebrations, care committees, staff circles, etc.) and do little or nothing to assess or nurture the health of their workplace culture. When school's lack inclusion safety, teachers feel more isolated and stressed. In turn, they are unable to collectively build and sustain a school culture that welcomes all students. I have observed that in schools that lack inclusion safety, students are as likely to be labeled, excluded, blamed, and scapegoated as the teachers.

The second red flag April mentioned was that when her students began making academic progress, she received skepticism and criticism from other teachers rather than encouragement, congratulations, or a desire to share strategies. "We had to do these quarterly literacy assessments," April explained. "And my students were the only ones showing growth by the end of first quarter. By midyear it was clear that most of my students were on track to end the school year reading at or above grade level. When I presented the data at my grade-level team meeting, the only response I got was, 'Beginner's luck. You got an easy group of kids this year.' That was a lie." One of the kindergarten teachers had told me that at the end of the previous school year, the first grade teachers had made a list of all the "bad kindergartners" and refused to teach them. They demanded that these students be given to whoever the new teacher was going to be, which in this case was me." April said, "It got worse as the year went on. Anytime my students showed progress, I could feel the resentment. I got tired of the side-eyed looks, the backhanded compliments, and the pettiness. When my students would make learning gains, I'd celebrate it with them and downplay it with my colleagues."

Psychologically unsafe schools lack learner safety, meaning that teachers are subject to ridicule for engaging in professional learning and growth. We will discuss learner safety, the second stage of psychological safety, in greater detail in Chapter 5; however, for now it is important to understand that in psychologically unsafe schools, every stage of the learning process is stifled. In these schools, teachers are as likely to be punished for asking questions or making mistakes as they are for achieving success. The teacher or team whose students excel is a threat to the status quo. If a teacher shares about student progress, they run the risk of being perceived as bragging to make the other teachers look bad. As a result, teachers whose students make academic gains often hide these successes from colleagues to avoid criticism, envy, or derision. This lack of learner safety prevents teachers from sharing strategies, learning from and with one another, and collectively improving their instructional practices. Students suffer from being taught by educators who stubbornly adhere to outdated instructional and behavioral approaches to avoid their own professional learning and evolution.

FEAR-BASED LEADERSHIP

April said that the third and most glaring red flag was that prior to her joining the staff, the school had three different principals over the course of 6 years. April told me that she was once at a district-wide professional development training and told the teacher sitting next to her the name of her school. The teacher responded, "Oh you work in the shark tank." April learned that her school had earned this nickname because her colleagues were notorious for ganging up on administrators until they fled.

April recalled the first staff meeting she attended at the school and feeling shocked by the blatant disrespect directed toward the principal. "First off, I remember some of the teachers had brought snacks for their table groups, which is great. But when the principal started talking, there were teachers who turned their backs to him and could be heard talking over him about salted caramel popcorn. He ignored it and kept going. Things eventually came to head when he was talking about a strategy for kindergarten literacy instruction. And this teacher says in front of everyone, 'You've never taught kindergarten. You don't know anything about how we should teach them.' Most of the teachers just nodded in agreement. And he didn't even try to defend himself."

April went on, "I was disappointed in him as a principal because he was afraid of the staff. He was good with the students, but as a building leader he was absent. He hid in his office all day except at recess, when you'd see him out playing with the kids. Meanwhile, for better or worse, the teachers were running the building." She shared one instance that stood out to her as an exception to the principal's pattern of avoidance and acquiescence. There was a third grade teacher who had moved a boy's desk to the back of her classroom because he was disruptive. The boy sat alone at his desk, while all the other students were seated together in table groups. The principal learned about this and asked the teacher to move the boy's seat back to one of the table groups. He offered to assist the teacher in developing a behavior plan to support the student. The teacher declined his offer and refused to move the boy's seat despite the principal visiting her classroom periodically to check in on the student.

"The teacher went to the district and filed a complaint against the principal alleging that his visitations to her classroom were acts of intimidation and harassment," April recounted, still visibly upset years after the ordeal. "A few other teachers, who were friends of hers, submitted statements in support of her allegations. One of the district's associate superintendents conducted an investigation and interviewed several of us, including the principal. The teachers' claims were ultimately dismissed because they weren't true, but their tactics worked. The principal never brought up the issue again. That teacher eventually decided to lock that boy out of her classroom every morning. He spent the last month of the school year doing worksheets in the front office. She wouldn't even give that child the chance to learn."

The pinnacle of psychological safety is challenger safety, the ability of a staff to address challenges and conflicts collaboratively and effectively. When schools lack psychological safety, the trust, vulnerability, and compromise needed to find solutions are out of reach. Instead, challenges escalate into conflicts that either fester as seething resentments or crescendo into all-out war; either of these unhealthy dynamics can be incredibly damaging to staff and students.

April suspected that the associate superintendent's investigation was the final straw for the principal. He began taking days off of work, which in retrospect, April assumed were to interview for other jobs. In May, the principal announced that he would not be returning the following school year. He had accepted a position at a school in a neighboring district. The school was now set to have its fourth principal in 7 years, but the next one wasn't going to be leaving anytime soon.

That summer, April was appointed to the hiring committee tasked with choosing the school's new principal. The hiring committee was made up of April, another teacher from her school, a building administrator from a different school, and three district administrators. Out of all the candidates who applied, the committee selected the candidate whom April felt was the least qualified based upon her credentials. Although April and her colleague had ranked this candidate as their last choice, all the district administrators had chosen her as their top pick, which resulted in her being offered the position. April was not surprised when she later learned that the candidate, soon to be her new principal, happened to be the sister-in-law of the district's superintendent.

"Things were bad from the beginning with her [the new principal]," April explained. "I remember in the beginning of the year, two of my students got into a fight during recess. So, I separate the two boys, and I walk them to the office. As soon as, they sit down in the front office, the principal comes out and says to me, 'Why are they here?' Before I finish telling her what happened, she says to me in front of the students, the office staff—there was even a father there waiting to pick up his child—'What were you thinking bringing them here? This is your problem. You handle it.' That was the moment that I knew things had gone from bad to worse."

April described in broad brush strokes the next 4 years of her life working at that school. April recounted times when she and colleagues were yelled at, belittled, and threatened. She described a workplace hijacked by fear, intimidation, and humiliation. "The worst part," April said, "was that as much as she made my life hell, some part of me still wanted to please her. One time she called me at midnight because asked me to compile data for a presentation she had to give at the district office the next morning. I stayed up all night getting it done. The next morning, she tells me that she had the dates of the presentation confused. She didn't even thank me. I put up with the thanklessness, the chaos, the contradictions for years. I knew that whatever I did was never going to be good enough for her, but I still wanted it to be."

I asked April how the other teachers responded to the principal. I expected to hear that they had banded together to get her fired or at least make her life so miserable that she'd search for a job elsewhere. However, I was wrong. "They didn't like her," April said, "but they feared her. She played their game better than they did. She had favorites, certain teachers who she always praised at staff meetings and whom she ate lunch with. She paid for them to go to conferences and trainings all over the country but declined other teachers' requests for PD [professional development]. She knew what she was doing. The teachers she favored—they were the biggest bullies among the staff. And the teachers she didn't like—she wouldn't hesitate to write us up. If she couldn't find a reason, she'd make one up. If a teacher was texting at a staff meeting while she was speaking, then you knew that teacher was going to be put on an improvement plan. The sad part was that she'd excuse teachers for cutting corners when it came to kids, just not when it came to her ego."

Psychologically unsafe schools are fear-based schools. They frequently have administrators who manage their schools with fear-based mindsets and practices. Some fear-based leaders attempt to become authority figures in their schools who engage in intimidation tactics to enforce compliance. Conversely, other fear-based leaders may be intimidated by their staff and resort to people pleasing and superficial expressions of gratitude and flattery to circumnavigate accountability and conflict. I have found that fear-based leadership styles can be characterized by the stress responses: fight, flight, freeze, and fawn.

Fear-Based Leadership Styles

<table>
<tr><th>Fight Behaviors</th><th>Flight Behaviors</th></tr>
<tr><td>

- Unfair and excessive criticism & blame
- Written and/or verbal insults
- Threats & intimidation
- Humiliation
- Favoritism
- Micromanagement
- Yelling and/or cursing at employees
- Unwarranted use of punitive measures to manage employee behavior
- Encouraging and rewarding individual staff members for "snitching" on colleagues
- Weaponizing walk-throughs, observations, & evaluations
- Narcissistic behaviors
- Retaliation
- Explosive outbursts

</td><td>

- Anxious disposition
- Excessive worry, overthinking situations & decisions
- Avoiding conflict, difficult conversations, & corrective action
- Frequently presenting staff with worst-case scenarios to scare them into action
- Perfectionism
- Workaholism
- Fluctuating between overwork & procrastination
- Looking for any opportunity to be out of the building, especially during times of conflict

</td></tr>
<tr><th>Freeze Behaviors</th><th>Fawn Behaviors</th></tr>
<tr><td>

- Physically present but emotionally & intellectually disengaged
- "Checked out" during meetings
- Numb, spacey, apathetic, and/or disconnected
- Isolating & avoiding others at work
- Difficulty making & communicating decisions
- Rarely present in classrooms or common areas throughout the school campus
- Rarely providing staff with guidance, feedback, or direction
- Allowing staff and/or students to control the school

</td><td>

- People pleasing
- Overly "nice" & resorting to flattery to avoid constructive feedback
- Lack of boundaries
- Performance evaluations of employees tend be excessively positive and lack an acknowledgment of growth areas
- Making excuses for staff rather than holding them accountable
- Overdeveloped sense of responsibility
- Frequently completing tasks that are the responsibility of other staff members
- Often contradictory communication because they frequently change their directives in an attempt to gain approval from others
- Easily manipulated

</td></tr>
</table>

I have found that fear-based leaders tend to rely predominantly on one of these four response types while occasionally borrowing behaviors from the other domains when useful. For example, a fear-based principal may primarily engage in fight behaviors such as excessive criticism and angry outbursts directed at staff. However, when a district administrator announces a visit to the school, the principal may utilize fawn strategies, resorting to excessive flattery and "love bombing" in an effort to win staff over prior to the visit.

A school administrator plays a crucial role in shaping the school's culture. These fear-based behaviors from a school leader can foster a fear-based culture that permeates the entire school. Staff are more likely to respond to a fear-based leader with their own range of fight, flight, freeze, or fawn behaviors. For example, April recalled teachers politely engaging with one another during meetings with their principal. However, she suspected that some of her colleagues would meet with the principal privately to throw their colleagues under the bus in effort to gain her favor.

April recounted a time when this happened to her, "The stress of working there was making me physically sick," she said. "One semester it was so bad that I developed irritable bowel syndrome. I had to rush to the bathroom several times a day, doubled over in pain. It was a nightmare because as teachers we don't even get the opportunity to pee during the school day. Thankfully, my classroom had an adjoining door with the classroom next to mine, so if you opened the door, you could stand in the doorway and observe the students in both classrooms. Most of the time, I just delt with the pain and waited until my students went to recess or specials to run to the restroom."

"One week, when my symptoms were at their worst, I explained my situation to the teacher in the classroom next to mine and asked her to watch my class from the doorway in case of a personal emergency. She agreed. She had to watch my class two times that week for maybe 5 minutes each time. The following Monday, in every teacher's mailbox was a letter from the principal saying that we are not allowed to leave students unattended in our classrooms under any circumstances, to do so will result in being written up and potentially terminated. The principal came up to me that day and asked if I had read the letter. At no point did I leave my students unattended, ever. But I am almost certain that that teacher went to her and said that's what I was doing." Accusations, scapegoating, and blame are common in schools where individuals want to make someone else the target of a hostile administrator's ire.

In a fear-based school, everyone must devote their energy to trying to stay safe, whether through isolation, banding together in cliques, or jockeying for status. The culture of the school lacks the psychological safety that is needed for the staff to effectively work together to meet the needs of their students. A fear-based school is a school that has lost its purpose. Self-preservation trumps collective efficacy. In the absence of a shared purpose, clear expectations, and structured collaboration processes, personalities take over; individuals endeavor to organize the school around their own priorities and agendas often to the detriment of students.

REFLECTION QUESTIONS

1. Have you ever worked in a school where the administrator frequently engaged in fear-based leadership behaviors? If so, how did that affect the ways that staff worked together?
2. How do educators in your school respond when a teacher shares an experience of success? What do you think this reveals about the level of psychological safety in your school?

FINDING PSYCHOLOGICAL SAFETY

I asked April what made her finally decide to apply for a teaching position in another district. "It was the summer after my fifth year teaching, and our school was hosting a summer enrichment program our district had launched that year. Given that it was its first year, it wasn't well attended, so they only needed a few teachers to run it. One night, I got a text from the office manager telling me that she was sick, and she wasn't going to be coming in to work for the rest of the week. That meant that if I needed to make copies or use the front office for any reason, it was just going to be me and my principal. The thought of being alone with her sent me into a panic. I know this sounds totally irrational, but I feared for my safety. I remember thinking to myself 'You're being absurd. She isn't going to hurt you.' But I couldn't shake the feeling. That was the moment I decided to look for a new job. I couldn't put up with that level of fear and anxiety anymore."

Throughout this book there are stories of individual educators and teams who foster psychological safety for themselves and their colleagues. There are also examples of school-wide initiatives that build psychological safety among all staff. However, April's story is one of a handful of stories included in this book that involves an educator leaving a school that has a toxic workplace culture to find a more psychologically safe work environment. As much as I might prefer to portray a more positive series of events, I chose to remain true to the real-life experiences that educators shared with me. The fact remains that schools lose amazing educators when they fail to support them.

The following week, a third grade position opened in a neighboring district. April applied and was eventually hired. April told me that despite feeling desperate to get out of her old school, she was cautious about accepting the new position. She knew from prior experience that bad can always get worse. After being offered the job, she asked the principal of her new school if she could talk to a couple of the staff members about their experiences working there. She also did research online, read comments from parents and families, and looked over the school's report card.

The principal got back to her the following day with the phone numbers of two teachers and a paraprofessional. Immediately, it seemed to April like a good sign that he included a paraprofessional, showing a consideration for equity of voice that hadn't existed at her old school. She asked the three staff member questions about their experiences working at the school. Overall, the majority of what she heard was positive. Certain themes came up in each of the conversations: the staff was committed to doing what was best for kids; they celebrated staff birthdays and major life events; they checked in on each other during times of illness or loss; time spent in professional learning communities (PLCs) was productive; the principal was liked and respected; staff felt appreciated by their administrator and one another; teachers who were new to teaching were assigned a mentor, and teachers who transferred from other schools were assigned a buddy teacher their first year; and the special education and general education staff collaborated regularly. These are all indicators of a school with a high degree of psychological safety where staff felt connected, supported, and valued.

Unsurprisingly, April's soon-to-be new school also had a higher rate of staff retention than her previous school. New teachers typically lasted 2–3 years at April's last school. However, April's new school had lower rates of absenteeism and turnover among staff. This trend is not surprising given what researchers have found about the influence of psychological safety across a variety of professional fields. Staff retention is a by-product of psychological safety. Research has shown that psychological safety reduces emotional exhaustion, work-related stress, and burnout, all of which reduce efficacy and fuel staff turnover.[2] Feeling like a valued member of a team is both less stressful and more rewarding than working in an environment where you feel isolated, overwhelmed, targeted, and exploited. Psychologically safe workplaces have been shown to elicit greater employee engagement, organizational loyalty, and job satisfaction.[3] When staff feel psychologically safe, they invest more of themselves into their work, and they are happier doing it. In psychologically safe schools, students benefit from having teachers who are more present, invested, and resilient.

Given the positive qualities of April's new school, I was surprised to learn that after accepting the position, she felt "thankful and worried." She said, "I kept thinking as soon as my principal finds out that I'm leaving, she's going to retaliate in some way, and this opportunity will get taken away from me. Fortunately, that didn't happen, at least not right away. When I told her that I was not going to be returning the following year, she gave me the silent treatment for the remainder of that school year."

However, April was not spared from her previous administrator's wrath. April shared, "About a month into working at my current school, I received an email from my former principal. She claimed that three laptops were missing from the laptop cart that I had used during the summer program. In the email, she asked if I might have taken them with me when I packed up my classroom. She even called my new principal and asked him if he had seen the laptops. He confided in me that he had to stifle his laughter when telling her no. Apparently, she ended the call by telling him to keep an eye on me."

"This time, I wasn't going to tolerate her antics," April continued. "I called HR at my previous district and asked to file a complaint. I told them about how she treated me when I worked at her school. I forwarded them the email she sent me about the laptops. I told them about the call to my current administrator. I also sent them a copy of the materials spreadsheet that I had saved when I left that school. The spreadsheet showed that all the materials assigned to my classroom, including the laptop cart, had been returned in full. The spreadsheet was signed by the office manager and the principal. The HR representative promised to keep me informed about the status of my complaint. I never heard back from them, but more importantly, I never heard from her again. She's still the principal of that school though."

Fear of retaliation was a common theme in conversations I had with educators who had been the target of workplace bullying. Educators shared about retaliatory behaviors that included but were not limited to verbal and written abuse, social exclusion, silent treatment from colleagues, negative evaluations from administrators, and even vandalism of personal property. I have found that the threat of retaliation is enough to coerce many educators into relinquishing their personal and professional boundaries, especially boundaries that define either how they are willing to be treated or which tasks they are responsible for completing at work. Educators are forced to decide whether establishing a boundary is worth the pushback they will encounter. If the response to the boundary is likely to be extreme and harsh, then establishing that boundary poses a greater risk than continuing to endure mistreatment.

April discussed her emotionally poignant decision to assert her self-worth and leave her former school. "The thing that I still think about after all these years is why I stayed at my old school for as long as I did." April shared, "I think part of it is that I loved my students. I genuinely cared about them and their families. In some ways, deciding that I deserved to be treated better felt like I was turning my back on them. I felt guilty when I left that school. I was also angry at myself for letting that principal and some other teachers treat me the way they did. Since I left, I've had to forgive myself for not standing up for myself sooner. I've also promised myself that I will never put up with that kind of abuse again. I will leave."

I asked April if the administrator of her current school has a different leadership style than the previous one. She responded with an emphatic, "Yes!" She then went on, "First off, he cares about us. When my son broke his arm, he checked in to see how he was healing. Also, he listens to us. When he has a big decision to make, he asks for our input. And, when he shares his decision, he explains why he made it and how it connects back to our purpose."

When it comes to decision-making, her administrator's invitation for input and open communication builds trust and a sense of shared responsibility among the staff. His transparency also quelches any gossip that would normally arise if there were an absence of clarity. Also, whether they agree with his decisions or not, they know what to expect, and that allows them to feel a sense of security. In schools where staff are subject to contradictory whims and abrupt changes without warning, they often develop a persistent fear of having the rug pulled out from under them. When staff are afraid in this way, they are more likely to cling to the status quo and carry out substandard directives without challenge. Dogged compliance is the lowest common denominator in schools and fails to produce the collaboration and innovation that are necessary for educational excellence.

I asked April how her administrator navigates conflict because her previous administrators tended to be either avoidant (flight/freeze) or domineering (fight). "I think he tries to lead by example," April explained. "When he says he's going to do something, he does it. On the rare occasion when he doesn't follow through on his word, he doesn't pretend like it didn't happen. He apologizes and takes action to repair the situation. Leading with that level of humility and integrity sets the tone for the rest of the staff."

She added, "To be clear, he has high expectations for us. This is not an easy place to work; we are expected to fulfill our promise to kids. If a subgroup of students falls behind, you bet he will be at our PLCs working right along with us to figure out what we can do to improve. And he doesn't let teachers get away with not doing their jobs. He recently fired a teacher who received multiple complaints from parents about how she spoke to students. He gave her coaching and multiple chances to improve, but she was stuck in her ways. I hate to see someone get fired, but I like working in a building where staff are accountable to the kids and one another."

CONNECTED AND FIRM LEADERSHIP

April's current administrator has a leadership style that is connected and firm rather than fear based. He cultivates positive relationships with his staff while maintaining a culture of integrity and accountability. Her administrator listens to his staff, invites their input as needed, responds to their concerns, advocates on their behalf when appropriate, and offers care and grace when they are struggling. At the same time, he holds himself and his staff accountable to their shared purpose, commitments, and professional responsibilities. A connected and firm leadership style fosters psychological safety through this balance of empathy and accountability.

One of the reasons administrators engage in fear-based behaviors is because of the lack of support and professional development that they receive within their districts. Being a school administrator can be incredibly demanding, stressful, and isolating, especially for principals who do not have an assistant principal or any other administrative personnel in their school. Not to mention: staff members can provoke fear-based responses from their school administrator when they lie, bully, or repeatedly fail to follow through on their professional responsibilities, all of which diminish the administrator's experience of trust and safety. If we want to see school administrators behave in ways that are connected and firm, then districts need to provide administrators with ongoing professional development and support. School districts must provide all administrators with opportunities to learn about psychological safety and develop their skill sets to create inclusive school environments, facilitate equitable and productive collaboration, provide supportive accountability, and resolve conflict. School staff members also need to offer their administrators empathy and grace, understanding each of us has unique strengths and growth areas and that we are stronger together. Later in this book, we will discuss individual and collective accountability, which are also essential for a psychologically safe workplace for all staff, including administrators.

It is important to keep in mind that although we've explored the significant influence that administrators have on school culture, they are not the sole influence. A school's culture is co-created by the administration, staff, students, families, and the greater community. Unless an administrator is founding a new school, they typically encounter an established school culture that they must learn and navigate. Many schools also have informal leaders, individuals (who are not administrators) who staff confide in, seek advice from, and rely on to resolve problems. I once worked in a school where teachers were far more likely to go to the school counselor for help with a problem than the principal. In turn, the counselor would act as an intermediary, negotiating a resolution with the administrator on behalf of the teachers. In many respects, the principal wasn't the one running the building; the staff was far more likely to look to the school counselor for direction. All of this is to say this that it is important to remain mindful of the influence that all stakeholders have in shaping a school's culture, especially administrators and staff.

Connected and Firm Leadership Behaviors

- Knows every staff member by name
- Regularly seeks input from multiple stakeholders
- Frequently expresses empathy and appreciation
- Follows through on job responsibilities, promises, and commitments
- Is frequently present in classrooms and common areas throughout the campus
- Works with staff to implement school-wide collective care practices that support staff well-being and resilience
- Admits when they make a mistake, fail to follow through on a commitment, or behave in a way that erodes trust and takes action to repair situations and relationships as needed
- Listens and responds to staff members' needs, even when it means telling staff "no" because a need or request cannot be met at that time
- Conducts walk-throughs, observations, and evaluations in ways that build trust and facilitate professional learning and growth
- Maintains appropriate professional boundaries within staff relationships and avoids playing favorites, gossiping, or people pleasing
- Exhibits a growth mindset and professional learning behaviors (e.g., admits when they don't know something, researches best practices, asks questions, continually develops their knowledge and skills as a leader, etc.)
- Communicates as transparently as possible regarding decisions that affect the staff
- Respectfully navigates conflict with the intention that all parties feel heard and that the conflict is resolved in a way that fosters mutual understanding and, if possible, a win-win outcome
- Is willing and able to mediate conflicts that occur between staff members if needed
- Provides supportive accountability (e.g., articulates shared goals, maintains high expectations for staff, provides constructive feedback, establishes collaboration protocols, ensures that school-wide practices are implemented with fidelity, etc.)
- Engages in corrective action (e.g., staff improvement plans, disciplinary actions, etc.) when staff members significantly and/or repeatedly violate the employee code of conduct or fail to fulfill their professional duties

REFLECTION QUESTIONS

1. How would working in a psychologically safe school positively affect you and your colleagues?
2. Have you ever worked in a school that had an administrator who exhibited a connected and firm leadership style? If so, how did that affect the ways that staff worked together?

WE AREN'T PERFECT, BUT WE DO OUR BEST

I asked April how she felt about working with the other teachers at her current school. "I'm happy here," she said. "We aren't perfect, but we do our best. At the start of every meeting, we read our mission and values. And, at the end of the meeting, we ask ourselves: Have we made decisions that are in the best interest of our students? Have we considered the needs of all our students? How will we know the impact of the decisions we've made? Reflecting on our purpose in that way helps me set aside the frustrations that inevitably arise from working with other people. I'm reminded that when we work together, we have a greater impact." A shared purpose is especially important in times of challenge when the psychological safety of a staff is tested.

"This was a tough year for us," April shared. "Our students struggled coming back to school after sheltering in place because of the COVID-19 restrictions. Then the district implemented a new mathematics curriculum for elementary schools. The new curriculum doesn't align with our old one; there are some significant gaps, which quickly revealed themselves in our assessment data as gaps in student achievement. At my old school, those achievement gaps would have persisted and worsened because teachers would have spent the entire year blaming the district for purchasing a subpar curriculum. At my current school, we use guiding questions in our PLCs that keep the focus on us and what we can control as educators, which helps us avoid getting stuck in blame. Once we realized that the new curriculum wasn't meeting our needs, we understood the issue was bigger than any single grade-level team, so we came together as a whole staff. We met in horizontal and vertical teams and developed supplementary units to fill in the gaps in our current curriculum. It was a lot of work, but our efforts paid off because our students showed considerable growth."

The ability of April and her colleagues to productively address the gaps they uncovered in both the mathematics curriculum and student learning outcomes is evidence of a high degree of psychological safety. Research has shown that psychological safety facilitates professional learning and growth. Studies have shown that when a workplace is psychologically safe, staff are more likely to engage in reflective learning processes, communicate openly, seek feedback from one another, and explore ways to improve.[4] Professional learning and growth pave the way for another important by-product of psychological safety—innovation.

Psychologically safe teams encourage creativity and risk-taking and embrace mistakes and failures as opportunities to learn, all of which are critical for innovation.[5] The ability of a team to innovate is especially important in education because I have never known a single curriculum or strategy to work for every student. For example, a curriculum might fail to account for the needs of emerging language learners, or a classroom management strategy may further dysregulate students on the autism spectrum. Identifying these "failures" opens up the possibility for innovation. As we saw with April's school, they bypassed blame and moved into action. They created the curricular materials that their students needed to progress. Making sure that each student gets what they need to be successful in school is at the heart of educational equity.

It is worth mentioning that most students in April's current school have been affected by poverty and trauma. A large percentage of the students are immigrants or refugees who emigrated due to extreme poverty and violence in their countries of origin. In the United States, many of their families continue to struggle to make ends meet, confronted with a lack of affordable housing, limited employment opportunities, and a myriad of linguistic and cultural barriers. However, by the time students at April's school complete fifth grade, the majority meets or exceeds grade-level standards in mathematics and language arts. In fact, April's school is one of the highest-performing schools in her district and the recipient of multiple state and national awards.

At the close of our conversation, April added, "See what I know now that I didn't know when I started teaching is that one of the biggest differences between a low-performing school and a high-performing school isn't the students; it's how well the educators work together." This last point of April's is central to the purpose of this book. For too long, professional development for educators has focused on "fixing the kids" rather than creating the conditions that enable educators to be effective. In fact, strategies do not transform schools; effective systems do. Effective systems are built through teamwork that is guided by evidence of impact. Psychological safety establishes the conditions needed for educators to collaborate in productive and impactful ways that build our individual and collective efficacy.

LESS FEAR, GREATER IMPACT

As you may recall from Chapter 1, collective teacher efficacy is one of the greatest influences on student achievement. Collective efficacy mitigates the harmful effects that poverty, prior learning gaps, ACEs and trauma, and a lack of parental involvement have on learning (if you would like to learn more about collective efficacy, see the Additional Resources at the end of this book). Collective efficacy is the shared belief among educators that when they work together, they can positively affect student outcomes.

I am going to propose an idea that may be controversial to some, which is that when we define collective efficacy solely as a shared belief, we run the risk of reducing it to a matter of mindset. This is an especially dangerous trap given how much energy we waste trying to inspire and maintain the ever elusive "buy-in" that we hope will transform our schools. When in fact, researchers, educators, and thought leaders have pointed to enabling conditions that cultivate collective teacher efficacy, including constructive feedback among staff, responsive leadership, teachers' experiences of success, and structured collaboration cycles.[6] Therefore, I propose that we think of collective teacher efficacy as the implementation of enabling conditions that facilitate educators' professional learning and their implementation of practices that produce measurable gains in student achievement. This shifts our focus from mindsets to practices and systems. Don't get me wrong; a shift in mindset is transformative. Changing our own mindset is hard enough; getting someone else to buy in to a new mindset is exceedingly difficult. However, educators don't have to "buy in" when they *know* that the practices that they've implemented have improved student outcomes.

Let me offer an analogy to illustrate my point. Let's say that I want to lose weight. I decide to eat healthier foods and exercise regularly. Now, I am going to be completely honest with you; I'm vegan, and I hate salads. I even have mixed feelings about vegetables. My favorite vegan food group is dark chocolate. Also, I don't like to exercise. I don't run, not even for my life. So, when I start this diet and exercise program, my mindset is fairly negative. In fact, I've tried to diet before and failed, so I'm not even particularly hopeful. However, this time around, I decide to try some new strategies (e.g., high-intensity interval training, healthy recipes I enjoy, etc.). After a few weeks, I start seeing results. I feel stronger and less fatigued, and the numbers on the scale are going down. Guess what also starts to change? My mindset. I feel empowered. I know I can do hard things. Maintaining my diet and exercise program is now worth it to me because I'm seeing results.

First, I identified a problem and a goal. Then I changed my behavior despite my disempowering and negative beliefs. Then I saw results, and finally my mindset shifted. The last thing to change was my beliefs. When we focus on trying to first change educators' beliefs, or cultivate buy-in, we put the cart before the horse. We know that our schools have growth areas and pain points. We know that the staff want things to be better. We also know that if we keep doing the same things we've always done, we will get the same results. Thankfully, we now also have more research than we have ever had in the history of education that can help us identify evidence-based practices to address the needs of our students. We also have each other and the wisdom that is present within ourselves and our colleagues. All we need is a process that moves us into action and keeps us focused on results.

When April spoke about the guiding questions that structure her current school's PLCs, she was referring to a collective efficacy cycle. Collective efficacy cycles are an essential enabling condition for cultivating collective teacher efficacy. Within a collective efficacy cycle, educators take action, collect and analyze data, and celebrate small wins that, with time and sustained effort, turn into major achievements.

A collective efficacy cycle is comprised of steps that facilitate collaboration, action, and impact. A typical collective efficacy cycle guides a team through creating a common goal, learning new strategies, implementing these strategies, collecting and analyzing data, and celebrating progress while refining their goals and practices as needed.[7] Within these steps, thought leaders and educators have embedded guiding questions, protocols, and resources to support educators in identifying common challenges, analyzing student work, researching evidence-based strategies, and piloting new practices. Regardless of how robust or nuanced you make these steps, one thing remains true: A team cannot effectively navigate a collective efficacy cycle without psychological safety.

Collective Efficacy Cycle

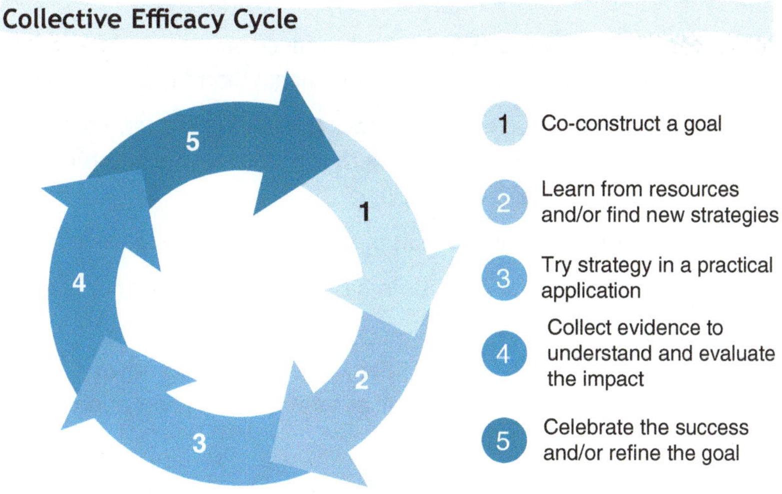

Look over the steps within a collective efficacy cycle, and ask yourself, can a team accomplish these if its members don't trust one another? When their administrator engages in fear-based behaviors that expose them to greater interpersonal risks? If team members repeatedly harm each other through workplace bullying? If team members are ridiculed for speaking up with new ideas that challenge the status quo? If the team's collaborative process lacks structure to the point where their conversations quickly devolve into blame, defensiveness, and criticism? Educators cannot achieve collective efficacy when they don't feel safe enough to share their ideas, questions, and concerns. Collective teacher efficacy requires psychological safety.

REFLECTION QUESTIONS

1. How does fear affect learning? How does psychological safety support professional learning?
2. How does psychological safety help educators develop collective efficacy?

KEY TAKEAWAYS

- Psychological safety has been shown to reduce burnout and increase job satisfaction, productivity, and professional learning among staff.
- The four stages of psychological safety (inclusion, learner, contributor, challenger) build upon one another while remaining interconnected and mutually reinforcing.
- Some practices help develop multiple stages of psychological safety.
- An administrator's leadership style has a significant influence on all stages of psychological safety.
- Fear-based leaders exhibit fight, flight, freeze, and/or fawn behaviors that diminish psychological safety and collaboration among staff.
- Connected and firm leaders cultivate psychological safety and collective efficacy through empathy and accountability.
- Collective teacher efficacy is defined as the shared belief among educators that they can improve student outcomes.
- Collective efficacy is one of the greatest influences on student achievement. Collective efficacy lessens the negative effects that poverty, ACEs and trauma, lack of parental involvement, and gaps in prior achievement have on learning. In schools with high levels of collective efficacy, students make significant learning gains, often achieving more than a year's worth of learning in a year's time.
- Collective efficacy is built through enabling factors and conditions including self-care, responsive leadership, teachers' experiences of success, constructive feedback among staff, and structured processes for collaboration (e.g., protocols, collective efficacy cycles, coaching cycles, etc.).
- By implementing school-wide practices and conditions that facilitate collective efficacy, we improve student outcomes and expand educators' mindsets.
- A collective efficacy cycle is a structured collaborative process through which teams identify a common challenge and goal, increase their knowledge and skills, implement and refine pedagogical practices according to evidence of impact, celebrate progress, and continually improve.
- To be effective, each step of a collective efficacy cycle requires psychological safety.

PRACTICES, STRATEGIES, AND TOOLS

Individual Educator
• We are still early on in our psychological safety learning journey. For now, simply notice the types of leadership behaviors that are exhibited in your school and how they shape workplace culture. • Notice the degree to which psychological safety is present in the ways that you and your colleagues communicate and collaborate.
Team
• If your team is focused on improving student outcomes, compare your collaboration process with the collective efficacy cycle. Identify any ways that the structure of your team's collaboration process could be improved. • Notice the degree to which psychological safety is present in the ways that team members communicate and collaborate with one another. • Invite team members to notice how they respond when someone shares either a challenge or a success.
Administrator
• Identify the practices and conditions within your school that facilitate collective teacher efficacy. • Identify any practices or conditions within your school that diminish collective efficacy. • Reflect on your leadership style and the degree to which you engage in fear-based versus connected and firm leadership behaviors. Notice the impact these behaviors have on staff and workplace culture. • Seek support within your district, and advocate for your needs. The first place you may find support is from other administrators in your district. • Look over the list of Connected and Firm Leadership Behaviors in this chapter. Identify which ones are strengths or growth areas for you. Choose at least one of the behaviors to practice more often.

INCLUSION SAFETY

SOCIAL GROUP DYNAMICS

You may recall that in Chapter 1, we met Jayda, a high school math teacher who was being gossiped about and socially excluded by colleagues. Jayda's school was run by a hierarchy of social cliques with clear insiders and outsiders. Her school's principal played favorites by primarily listening to a small group of teachers who were also friends with the administrator. This influential group of teachers included the chair of Jayda's department, who influenced decisions that affected the entire school and shaped the ways that individual teachers were treated and evaluated by the administration.

Having friends and a healthy sense of belonging in the workplace is important. A sense of inclusion safety at work has a positive impact on everything from job performance to retention rates. Problems arise, however, if workplace relationships cause harm to others, as in the case with Jayda's school. Now, we don't know how teachers in Jayda's school found themselves fractioned off into cliques. Perhaps it happened naturally over time as teachers formed relationships with the colleagues that they spent the most time with or shared the most in common with. However, the culture of the building became toxic because a certain group was afforded more power and influence than colleagues with whom they should have shared equal footing.

The tricky thing about social cliques is that although they offer members of the group a relative sense of safety, belonging, and support, they also offer power, which can be exerted in ways either helpful or harmful. Positive peer pressure within a group can motivate members to engage more fully, put effort into achieving common goals, and show up for each other in times of struggle. Negative peer pressure pushes members to conform out of the fear of being targeted or excluded, thereby eliminating any sense of inclusion safety. Groups can also exert power over other groups and individuals, especially in work environments where priorities compete, decisions need to be made, and finite resources must be allocated.

If your school's teaching staff can be easily organized into small social groups, and if you happen to be a member of one or more of these groups, I want to invite you to reflect upon two factors: shared identity and power. When I speak of shared identity, I'm simply referring to the common characteristics of each group. Shared identity is often determined by some criteria for inclusion. In other words, what characteristics does an individual need to possess (or not possess) to become a member of a group. For example, do teachers in your school tend to group themselves by age, race, country of birth, body size, gender, sexual orientation, socioeconomic status, ability or disability, and/or first language? Or are teachers more likely to bond with those who share the same grade level, content area, or years of professional experience? Are there still other traits or interests that tend to define the groups within your school?

In schools with a high degree of inclusion safety, individuals and groups affirm and respect diverse identities and navigate conflict in ways that share power and arrive at mutually beneficial outcomes and/or best practices. I was working with a middle school where the staff could be almost evenly divided between staff whose first language was Spanish and staff whose first language was English. Within each department, social groups had formed along these lines. In other words, the people whose first language was Spanish tended to eat lunch together, chat in the hallways, and spend time together outside of work. When they socialized at work, they primarily spoke with one another in their first language. These same dynamics were true among the staff whose first language was English. These criteria for inclusion into either of these two social groups was someone's primary language.

All criteria for inclusion carry certain benefits and costs. There are certainly benefits to communicating with other people who share your first language in a multilingual setting. For example, it's easier to speak and understand one another. Idioms, colloquialisms, metaphors, and humor are more likely to be understood, and there is a greater likelihood for shared cultural references. However, there can also be drawbacks and challenges that professionals encounter in a multilingual workplace, such as misunderstandings, miscommunication, and even social division and exclusion because it is easier to talk with someone who shares your primary language rather than do the work of translating for yourself or another person.

As for the middle school I mentioned, some of the teachers who knew how to speak only English complained that their colleagues were being "unprofessional" when they spoke to one another in Spanish. A few of the monolingual English-speaking teachers said that they feared their colleagues were gossiping about them and making jokes about them in Spanish. These allegations could have easily divided the entire staff further, causing considerable pain and disrupting professional collaboration.

However, this school chose to do something remarkable; they chose to address the problem in a productive and respectful forum. A few staff members asked that a staff meeting be dedicated to unpacking this issue, and the administration granted their request. The teachers facilitating the session began by reviewing communication agreements that were intended to keep the conversation respectful and professional. The conversation that followed wasn't easy because people shared perspectives that were rooted in strong emotions.

On the one hand, teachers expressed fear that they were being made fun of, disrespected, and excluded, and this fear reinforced defensive viewpoints about the "way things should be." On the other hand, many teachers expressed how valuable it felt for them to work in a place where other people spoke Spanish. One staff member said, "Sometimes I feel like I am holding my breath all day, and then I get to speak to someone in Spanish. I don't have to do the mental work to translate everything. It is like I finally get to exhale."

To help the staff navigate the conversation in a way that would be more authentic and productive, everyone was given a handout that listed emotions and needs based upon Dr. Marshall Rosenberg's Theory of Nonviolent Communication (NVC). NVC is an approach to communication and conflict resolution through which individuals communicate observations, feelings, needs, and requests (see the chapter on challenger safety for more on NVC).[1] This school happened to have two staff members who were trained in facilitating NVC. NVC is not the only, nor always the best, tool for organizations to use in navigating conflict; however, it helped this school address a complex issue in ways that strengthened inclusion safety. Let's explore how they applied the principles of NVC to arrive at a mutually beneficial outcome and a greater sense of belonging among staff.

When speaking, staff were asked to share what they were feeling and what need was or was not being met. Most of the staff expressed needs for respect and belonging, which evoked an array of emotions. Some staff members felt fear and anger because they perceived colleagues speaking in a language different from theirs as a threat to their social safety and status. Conversely, the experience of connection, belonging, and mutuality evoked equally strong emotions of joy, security, and gratitude among those who got the opportunity to talk with another colleague in their first language of Spanish.

These strong emotions reinforced several perspectives, some of which were inaccurate and biased. Facilitators reminded their colleagues that being multilingual is an asset in any professional setting, especially a school that serves many students and families who speak Spanish as their primary language. Second, there is nothing "unprofessional" about speaking your first language at work if the content is respectful and appropriate. The task remained for the staff to reach agreements on how to communicate with one another in ways that would meet their needs for connection and respect while understanding that this would require some compromise.

The staff developed an agreement that regardless of the language being spoken, every staff member engaged in a workplace conversation needed to have the opportunity to understand the content of the conversation. Putting this agreement into action would take translating (if necessary), pausing to allow think time during meetings, and periodically asking if anyone had clarifying questions. These moves would ensure full and equitable participation for everyone involved. Over time, several changes took place among the staff and their communication dynamics. Conversations during meetings felt less rushed, and the level of engagement and analysis deepened. New relationships started to form between teachers who had rarely spoken to each other in the past. Some of the teachers began to soften their defensive beliefs about speaking only English at school. These staff members said they felt more included in conversations but also humbled by having to ask clarifying questions as a monolingual speaker. They also started to express more empathy for parents, caregivers, and students who did not speak, or were learning to speak, English. As a whole, this school's staff were able to reach a common agreement that benefited the entire school community by strengthening practices of inclusion.

This scenario could have resulted in a different outcome had it not been handled with considerable intention, care, and professionalism. I can easily imagine the same topic coming up during a staff meeting and it being glossed over, only to fester, or being dealt with in a harmful and all-or-nothing attempt to ban other languages and vilify multilingual staff members. Instead, the staff worked together in a way that fostered inclusion safety by honoring feelings and needs and developing, through compromise and collaboration, mutually beneficial shared agreements. This brings me to second aspect of shared identity that I mentioned earlier: power. This school had two predominant social groups that chose to share power rather than attempt to exert power over one another and in doing so created a greater sense of inclusion safety.

REFLECTION QUESTIONS

1. Do teachers in your school organize themselves into different social groups? If so, do these groups share power with one another or try to exert power over each other?
2. Think about a challenging situation you are facing at your school. What emotions do you feel about the situation? What need(s) do you have that is(are) not being met when it comes to this situation? What would have to happen for this need to be met?

DIVISIVE POLITICS HARM SCHOOLS

Recently, political affiliation has become an increasingly common criteria for inclusion. Educators have forged as well as destroyed relationships with one another based upon their politics. Many politicians, pundits, social media influencers, and media outlets have fueled this "tribalism" by framing political parties as opposing sides of a culture war. Dialogue and debate have been replaced by sound bites, sensationalism, fearmongering, and trash-talking. These media stunts and distractions provide cover for many politicians to routinely fail to address the needs of the people they are elected to serve.

In 2020, I provided virtual professional development sessions to more than 30,000 educators across the United States from the East to the West Coast (and Hawaii), Alaska to the United States-Mexico border, "Red" to "Blue" states, and communities in between. Educators shared about feeling overwhelmed, afraid, stressed, frustrated, and pushed to previously unknown levels of burnout. They had to navigate wildly uncertain and changing territory, while the media and politicians planted landmines of misinformation to fuel fear and rage. Many state and federal leaders abandoned or attacked public schools. Elected officials abdicated their responsibilities, undermined medical guidance, and left public health decisions on the desks of school administrators. In effect, they set schools up to take the fall for their failure to lead. School principals and superintendents spoke to me about the anxiety of having to make life-and-death decisions regarding COVID-19 precautions with little guidance or support. Their jobs went from "you can't please everyone" to "you can't please anyone," knowing that they'd be hated (and at times have their lives threatened) for whatever choice they made.

I worked with one school district in which inclusion safety was eroded by educators who stopped speaking to one another because of their political beliefs. It started in 2020, when some expressed a belief that the pandemic was a hoax orchestrated by global elites. School board members who shared this belief struck down any attempt made by schools in the district to require facial coverings in school, even prior to the availability of a COVID-19 vaccine. On the other side of this issue, educators (and many students and parents) feared that attending school without a mask would guarantee exposure to a highly contagious and deadly virus. Animosity and division escalated to the point where members of the school board threatened to sue teachers who insisted on wearing face coverings at school.

Both sides of this issue felt that the other side was attempting to exert power over them. One side feared that a mask mandate would leave them alive but powerless. Powerlessness is an awful feeling, and for many it evokes fear, anger, and a desire to fight for one's own agency. Conversely, others feared contracting COVID-19 and being hospitalized on a ventilator, unable to see, touch, or speak to their loved ones. Being extremely sick evokes fear and a desire to fight for one's survival. But this school district didn't frame this as a dialogue around feelings and needs; instead they framed it as a battle in which there could be only one winner and one loser. It didn't help that every scientific fact about the virus was reframed as a conspiracy, making it almost impossible to agree upon some common ground. The result was that many educators, students, and families contracted COVID-19, and trust was broken across the school community.

I spoke to this district's superintendent and building administrators throughout the course of 2020 and 2021. They shared that in the aftermath of the 2020 presidential election, things had gotten so bad that divisions worsened, and many teachers had stopped speaking to colleagues who shared differing political beliefs. For their schools, the fear and anger that had typified 2020 had been replaced by cold, distant resentment and distrust among the staff.

As strange as this may sound, I don't blame the teachers of this district for their beliefs and behaviors, *partly* because I have heard similar stories, although not always to this scale, throughout the country and *mostly* because I value them for continuing to show up and teach through one of the most challenging times in our field. I also don't find fault with their school leadership for not setting a better tone. I have yet to hear of a graduate program that trains future school administrators to navigate public health data, misinformation campaigns, political unrest, and crisis-level conflict resolution during a global pandemic. This school district, and others like it, have experienced a significant breakdown in inclusion safety evidenced by division, power struggles, and a growing sense of animosity and mistrust among staff and within their larger community. I believe that for many educators, the persistent chaos, stress, and fear of the past couple of years has been a form of collective trauma that few have been given the opportunity to process.

To offer a real sense of hope, I want to uplift the schools and districts that have managed to develop inclusion safety through collaboration during these difficult times. Their educators express feeling more connected to one another, despite their political differences, because they supported each other through these times of challenge. In working with these schools and districts, certain trends emerged that when reflected upon give us valuable insight into ways to cultivate inclusion safety during times of crisis. These districts also reveal that inclusion safety is a necessity for delivering on our promise to do what is best for students. The pandemic has been one hurdle, but there will be many more, of varying degrees, to come. Reflecting on these practices now allows us to learn and grow from our trials so that we find ourselves stronger for having struggled.

First, administrators in these schools and districts articulated a clear set of priorities. During times of uncertainty and conflict, it is essential that we ground ourselves in a common purpose, which for schools means putting students first. As one administrator said to her staff at the beginning of shelter in place, "We will do three things. We will care for our students. We will care for ourselves. We will care for one another." This simple message clearly articulated a shared commitment to do what is best for students while also practicing self- and collective care. Throughout the next 2 school years, this message was shared again and again with staff, students, parents, school board members, and the larger community so that everyone was on the same page.

Next, school and district leaders listened to the feelings and needs of their staff, students, and families. This gave everyone the opportunity to feel heard rather than feeling as though they had to win an argument against their opponents. These administrators then considered what they heard and responded in ways that were both connected and firm: connected in the sense that there was reflection, consideration, and empathy for what was expressed by the members of their school community and firm in that the decisions they made were grounded in the priorities they had articulated and not swayed by factionalism, intimidation, or political jockeying.

For example, one superintendent had several staff members, parents, students, and school board members who were opposed to wearing facial coverings in school, even prior to the availability of a vaccine. She spoke to them about the district's commitment to do what was best for kids. She knew that meant having the students back in school, safely, as soon as possible. Despite their opposition to masks, these individuals wanted this as well. She explained that although masks can be a pain to wear (and some folks doubt their effectiveness), Centers of Disease Control and Prevention (CDC) guidance has been clear that facial coverings, social distancing, hand-washing, and other safety precautions prevent the spread of COVID-19. For schools to reopen, for them to have fewer quarantines, fewer absences, more in-class instruction, more school events, more school sports games and performances—more students seen, fed, taught, and cared for—then masks were going to be a necessity for the time being. Many of the individuals who were opposed to wearing masks saw that by compromising and following the CDC's guidance, they would be helping get students back in school as soon as possible, which was something they very much wanted.

However, among those who were vocal advocates for facial coverings, many were not in favor of reopening schools for in-person instruction prior to the availability of a vaccine. This was an especially difficult position for the superintendent to be in. She had spoken with grieving families of students and staff members who had lost loved ones to COVID-19. She listened as they pleaded for ongoing virtual instruction to prevent further illness and save lives. She acknowledged their pain and remained both empathic and rooted in the commitment to do what was best for students. She offered a compromise, which was that schools would reopen for in-person instruction in the fall of 2020, but students and some staff could opt into hybrid instruction from their homes.

During 2020 and 2021, the superintendent established an important boundary that protected her district from being hijacked by the chaos that had affected many neighboring school communities. She deferred to up-to-date credible public health research and did not open decisions about COVID-19 safety precautions to public debate. Some people were upset by this; however, by implementing all of the safety protocols prescribed by the CDC, including facial coverings in schools, her district had the lowest cases and the fewest quarantines and COVID-19-related absences among neighboring districts that had not implemented these protocols. So yes, although people may have had opinions about how things should be done, the actions taken were successful in achieving the common goal of having kids in school. This was something that the entire community could celebrate. It was also a victory for inclusion safety because to implement these practices, staff worked together across their political and ideological differences toward a common good. The superintendent had fostered an environment where staff could share power by each playing an important role in doing what was best for their students.

Sadly, many schools and districts across the country are seeing a rise in political sectarianism within their communities. People increasingly view members of opposing political parties as enemies and threats. Political discussions have become less about policies and more about discrediting the other party's humanity. Social scientist Eli J. Finkel and his colleagues have identified three core components of political sectarianism:

- Othering: *People who hold different political views are so different from us that we can't relate to them.*
- Aversion: *They aren't only different from us; they are unlikable, less intelligent, and untrustworthy.*
- Moralization: *They are morally bankrupt. We are good, and they are evil.*

These processes of othering, aversion, and moralization are sustained through the spread of misinformation, negative stereotypes, and vitriolic rhetoric.[2] Political sectarianism has destroyed relationships between educators, impeded collaboration, compromised the quality and availability of curricular materials, turned school board meetings into public spectacle, and prevented students from getting the care and instruction they deserve.

Inclusion safety requires us to resist the othering, aversion, and moralization of political sectarianism. We achieve inclusion safety by intentionally building positive relationships with people who are different from us, across many dimensions of difference, including political affiliation. Instead of othering people, inclusion safety involves us to get to know them and discover ways that we're connected. Rather than looking for reasons to dislike entire groups of people, inclusion safety encourages us to look for the good in others. Instead of moralizing so that we can feel self-righteous and superior, inclusion safety is built through humility, vulnerability, and a willingness acknowledge one another's feelings and needs. Schools need inclusion safety among staff because we must work together to meet the needs of our students. Each of us can play a role in resisting political sectarianism within our schools to prevent it from doing further harm to our students, colleagues, and communities.

Ways You Can Resist Political Sectarianism for a Healthier School and a Healthier Democracy

- Fact-check news stories and social media posts.
- Reflect on positive experiences that you have had with people who hold different political views.
- Respectfully correct misperceptions and misinformation when you hear them.
- Question your assumptions about people who hold different political beliefs
- Practice intellectual humility by asking questions and seeking to understand other peoples' perspectives.
- Discover what you share in common.
- Look for the good in others.
- Teach media literacy to students and colleagues.
- Be aware of social media algorithms. Notice if you are in a virtual echo chamber of similar stories, ads, and posts. Notice how these make you feel and what they want you to believe about yourself and other people.
- Acknowledge the ways that emotions and needs shape our political views.
- Be kind. Positive social interactions make a big difference.

REFLECTION QUESTIONS

1. Has divisive political discourse affected your school community? How so?
2. Imagine that you are working with a colleague, and this colleague expresses political views that are the opposite of yours. Could this create any barriers to effective collaboration between you and this colleague? If so, how could you overcome these barriers?

WORKPLACE BULLYING AMONG EDUCATORS

These examples of districts affected by political divisions show how the ways that groups attempt to exert power over or share power with one another have a significant effect on the psychological safety and well-being of the entire school community. However, these power dynamics do not have to be as significant as politically fueled divisions during a global health crisis to erode inclusion safety. Social groups exert power in many more subtle ways among their members as well as those outside of their group. Some groups distribute power more equitably among members, whereas others are governed by informal hierarchies. If you've seen the movie *Mean Girls*, there is a perfect example of a group with an inequitable distribution of power that has a clear leader, the character Regina George, who uses relational aggression to influence, manipulate, control, and harm others.[3] Some of those same patterns and behaviors show up in schools among the staff albeit often in ways that are more covert. In essence, the social dynamics of high school have never gone away; they've gotten more sophisticated as we get older. The consequences grew from "Do I need to find a new table to eat lunch at?" to "Do I need to find a new school to work at?" And that is the question that Jayda was ultimately forced to ask herself.

In the final weeks of Jayda's third year teaching, her students took their state assessments. On average, Jayda's students out-performed the other students in the school. In fact, Jayda's scores were some of the highest in the city and contributed to an increase in the school's overall report card rating as determined by their state's department of education. Perhaps out of a mix of jealousy and bias, or maybe fear that Jayda would want to unseat her as department chair, Jayda's department chair made efforts to assassinate Jayda's character and diminish her achievements. She spread rumors that Jayda's students had cheated and that Jayda had helped them. There was even an allegation made that Jayda had somehow gotten ahold of her students' answer sheets, erased incorrect responses in the multiple-choice section of the test, and bubbled in the correct ones.

The bullying behavior peaked during an end-of-year meeting with the principal and the math department. It was a tradition that the principal met with each department at the close of the year to review their end-of-year assessment data. During that meeting, Jayda's department chair doubled down on her accusations that Jayda's students had cheated on their state assessments. She argued that Jayda's relationships with her students was the reason they were so motivated to cheat. She asserted that Jayda's students viewed Jayda more as a friend than a teacher, so they found ways to give each other the answers because they didn't want to disappoint her. The final straw came when one of the other teachers in the department said, "You put a lot of effort into entertaining your students, but our job is to actually teach them. I don't have time to make up rap songs about math." At that point, Jayda looked at the principal who sat there doing and saying nothing. Jayda defended herself to no avail. She said, "I conduct an item analysis on every unit assessment to identify topics for me reteach. I then differentiate my instruction so that my students learn. However, I've never made up a rap song about math, not because there would be anything wrong with that, but rapping is not my forte. And to me that comment feels racist." Everyone at the meeting rallied in defense of the teacher who had made the statement. That teacher began to cry and left the meeting. The principal got up and left the room to console the crying teacher, which brought the meeting to a close.

The gossip, false allegations, microaggressions, racist statements, and behaviors that Jayda endured are all forms of discriminatory harassment and workplace bullying. According to a 2021 national survey by the Workplace Bullying Institute, approximately one out of three U.S. workers report experiencing workplace bullying, and one out of five workers report having witnessed a colleague being bullied at work.[4] Workplace bullying often goes unreported because it is harder to identify than more overt forms of workplace harassment or discrimination.

Common Forms of Workplace Bullying

- Gossiping
- Scapegoating
- Backstabbing
- Humiliation
- Excessive unfair criticism
- Biased-based comments and behaviors (e.g., microaggressions and micro-assaults)
- Undermining and/or sabotaging someone's work
- Repeatedly ignoring a coworker
- Intentionally withholding resources and/or information that are necessary for a colleague to do their job
- Taking credit for someone else's work
- Reporting false allegations about a colleague to their supervisor
- Repeatedly excluding a coworker from work-related meetings and events

Workplace bullying involves a power differential; however, that difference in power can be professional, social, physical, or emotional. Workplace bullying destroys inclusion safety and impedes the ability of educators to work together. Examples of workplace bullying in schools may include the following:

- A principal singles out a particular teacher with excessively negative and inaccurate evaluations and writes the teacher up for behaviors that they allow other staff to engage in.
- A teacher repeatedly ignores and belittles a paraprofessional who works with their students.
- A group of teachers gossip about and criticize a fellow teacher to the point where they don't feel comfortable leaving their classroom during the school day.
- A general education teacher regularly undermines their colleague, saying that their colleague doesn't work as hard because they teach special education.
- Two staff members monopolize the conversation at their weekly grade-level team meeting. They talk over and on behalf of the other members of the team, never allowing anyone else the opportunity to speak.
- A group of teachers submit false complaints to their district administration in an effort to get their principal fired.

Workplace bullying behaviors can occur in person and/or virtually via email, online platforms, text messaging, and so on. Bullying can happen between two coworkers or involve multiple staff members. Jayda experienced a form of workplace bullying commonly referred to as "mobbing," which is when a group of colleagues repeatedly mistreats a coworker.

To address the workplace bullying that she was experiencing, Jayda scheduled a meeting with her principal. She told her principal that she had left the previous meeting feeling offended, hurt, and unsupported. The principal responded by saying, "I'm surprised to hear that you feel unsupported. When I hired you, I told you how important it was to me that we have a diverse staff." Jayda responded, "Yes, you hired me, and I am a Black educator, but you have not supported me as a Black educator. During that meeting, the statements made about me and my students were unfounded and offensive. And you said nothing in my defense." The principal said, "I'm sorry to hear that you feel this way." With that she ended the conversation, leaving Jayda without consolation or recourse.

Jayda then scheduled a meeting with the district's director of equity. He was angered and disgusted by what he heard. Jayda felt validated and relieved that she was finally going to get some help in addressing this issue, but as the meeting drew to a close, it took a turn for the worse. He said to Jayda, "You mentioned that all of this has negatively affected your mental health and even your relationship with your wife." Jayda said, "Yes." He said, "I didn't realize you were gay. What advice can you give me because I have these other LGBT teachers in the district that aggressively promote their lifestyle in the classroom, and parents have complained. So, I've moved their kids to other teachers' classrooms, but how can I encourage these LGBT teachers to be less-" Jayda interrupted him, saying, "These teachers are no more 'aggressively promoting their lifestyle' than you are with that picture you have of your family on your desk. The teachers you're referring to are simply existing. Would you remove children from a classroom because parents complained about a teacher's race or religion?" He said, "Absolutely not. Children need to learn to respect different identities." "So do you," she said.

After that meeting, Jayda made the decision to look for a new job. The following school year, Jayda started a position at a high school in another district. Unfortunately, the new position required her and her wife to move, leaving behind a condo and neighborhood that they loved. Being in a new school didn't erase the emotional scars of having endured such a toxic work environment. Even though Jayda was welcomed into her new school community, it took a while for her to feel a sense of inclusion safety and trust. Thankfully, with time, positive relationships took root.

Workplace bullying behaviors can become forms of discriminatory harassment when employees are targeted specifically because of their race, color, age, sex (including gender and sexual orientation), disability, religion, genetic information, or national origin. These forms of harassment and discrimination are prohibited by federal law. If you are experiencing any of these forms of discrimination and/or harassment at work, take detailed notes documenting each instance. If it is safe for you to do so, contact your supervisor and/or your school district's Human Resources department to report the incident(s) and request that they investigate and take appropriate disciplinary action. Also, ask them to provide you with a letter stating their knowledge of your claim and their intent to investigate it. Human Resources departments are increasingly common in urban and suburban school districts; however, many small and rural districts may not have them. Whether your district has a Human Resources department or not, your employer is required to investigate claims of workplace harassment and discrimination. If you are a member of a union or professional association, they may also be a good source of support and guidance in navigating the situation. You may also benefit from seeking legal counsel from an attorney, especially if you fear that your employer may retaliate against you or fail to appropriately respond to your claim. You may also choose to file a charge of employment discrimination through the U.S. Equal Employment Opportunity Commission as well as any other state or local fair employment agencies.

A growing number of school districts across the country are adopting policies that explicitly forbid all forms of workplace bullying, not only the forms of harassment and discrimination currently prohibited by federal law. While writing this book, I have heard stories from many educators about being bullied about their weight, socioeconomic status, appearance, and a myriad of other factors. For example, one teacher said to me, "They [her colleagues] didn't start to treat me with respect until I lost weight."

She said that in the years prior to her weight loss, coworkers would often ignore her in the hallways when she'd say hello or good morning. Several times, she overheard them making negative comments, and even cruel jokes, about her body size. She went on, "After I began losing weight, buying new clothes, then other teachers started talking to me for the first time. It felt good to have my existence acknowledged, but it also hurts when the first time someone talks to you, after years of working in the same building, it's to 'compliment' you for losing weight."

I've heard similarly painful stories from educators who have been bullied because of bias about their age. Sharon is a veteran teacher with more than 30 years of teaching experience. She said to me, "It's true that I started teaching when education was very different. A lot of colleagues I started out with have retired. Others still show up for work physically, but their heart isn't in it anymore. However, I think that says less about our age and more about the system of education. To remain passionate about teaching, to continue to grow as an educator, I've had to learn two different skill sets: how to navigate the system on the one hand and how to be a good teacher on the other. You'd think those would be related, but they aren't." She added, "What hurts though is that after all these years, I have a lot of hard-earned wisdom and ways that I could help other teachers. But most of my younger colleagues treat me like a burden. I see the eye-rolls and annoyance in their faces when I have something to say at a meeting. I've heard them joke about my age. They call me 'the dinosaur' behind my back."

I have heard other stories of ageist bullying from younger teachers who have shared that they've been continually ignored by more veteran educators and told that because of their age, and newness to field, they have little of value to contribute. Meanwhile, if these teachers experience success, then the academic gains of their students are chalked up to them being the "young cool teacher" rather than evidence of their pedagogical efficacy. One of the challenging aspects of situations like this and other instances of workplace bullying is knowing how to respond to them. Addressing workplace bullying is a courageous and critical step in developing inclusion safety within a school. Whether we witness, perpetuate, or experience workplace bullying, we can play an important role in stopping the harm it causes us and others.

Ways to Address Workplace Bullying

If you witness workplace bullying . . .	If you are being bullied at work . . .	If you are a workplace bully . . .
• If it is safe for you to do so, speak up. You can use affective statements such as, "When you said ___, I felt ___, and I would appreciate it if you would ___." • Speak to the person who was bullied privately. Find out if there is anything you can do to support them. • Offer to support the person who was bullied if they choose to report the incident. Be prepared to give a statement about what you witnessed including the date, time, location, and persons involved. • If the person who was bullied does not feel comfortable reporting the incident, you may still need to report it to an administrator and/or Human Resources. • Find strength in numbers. If workplace bullying is a significant problem in your school, join with others who are tired of it. Commit to treat one another with respect, and agree to speak up, document, and report instances of workplace bullying.	• If it is safe for you to do so, speak up for yourself. You can use affective statements such as, "When you said ___, I felt ___, and I would appreciate it if you would ___." • Document all instances of workplace bullying including dates, times, locations, persons involved, and save any email/text communications. • Document your work performance. Some workplace bullies will submit false evaluations and complaints about the people they are bullying. Be able to prove that you fulfill your professional duties. • Research your school and district's code of conduct, employee handbook, and any related policies pertaining to professional behavior, harassment, and discrimination. • Report the incidents to your administrator and/or Human Resources. Seek legal counsel if needed. • Look for a new job if the bullying persists. • Seek therapeutic care and social support as needed.	• Stop all bullying behaviors. • Restrict your communication at work to appropriate topics and work-related matters. • Be aware of your tone, body language, words, and behavior. Communicate and act in ways that are respectful and professional. • Be aware of any circumstances (e.g., social situations, specific individuals, power differentials, etc.) that trigger your bullying behaviors. Come up with a plan for how to manage your emotions and behavior when these triggers are present. • If it would not cause further harm to your victims, you may wish to apologize and ask them what you can do to repair the harm caused by your behavior. Then do it. • Seek therapeutic care and social support as needed. You may wish to explore with a therapist the motivations, fears, insecurities, hurts, and/or bias-based beliefs that underly your bullying behaviors.

REFLECTION QUESTIONS

1. Have you witnessed, experienced, and/or engaged in workplace bullying? If so, how have these experiences affected you and the other people involved?
2. Imagine that you are a teacher in a grade-level team meeting. During the meeting, one of your colleagues makes an excessively harsh and demeaning comment about another teacher who is in the meeting. The comment was unprovoked and said aloud for everyone to hear.
   a. How would you respond?
   b. Now, imagine that you are the teacher who the comment was directed to. How would you respond?
   c. Imagine that you are the teacher who made the demeaning comment. What could you do to attempt to repair the harm caused by your comment?

THE MORAL IMPERATIVE OF INCLUSION SAFETY

In the words of Timothy Clark, "Inclusion safety allows us to gain membership within a social unit and interact with its members without fear of rejection, embarrassment, or punishment, boosting confidence, resilience, and independence. But what if you're deprived of that basic acceptance and validation as a human being? In short, it's debilitating. It activates the pain centers of the brain. Granting inclusion safety to another person is a moral imperative."[5] Research has shown that threats to inclusion and belonging activate similar stress response systems in the brain, metabolic, and nervous systems that are activated by the threat of physical harm.[6] The brain is wired to treat belonging as a necessity for survival.

When Jayda spoke to her building and district administrator about the pain she experienced because of workplace bullying, she was referencing a pain that was both emotional and physiological. Rejection, exclusion, bullying, and other attacks against our sense of social safety activate the regions of the brain associated with physical pain.[7] When these regions of the brain are activated, functioning in the prefrontal cortex and limbic system is dysregulated, thereby reducing our capacity for concentration, problem-solving, communication, and memory. The amygdala becomes hyper-aroused in these painful moments, making us prone to distorted thinking and escalated emotional states. We become more likely to experience negative emotions; engage in all-or-nothing thinking; make snaps judgments based on cognitive heuristics, biases, and emotion; and even engage in fight, flight, freeze, or fawn behaviors. We might respond to workplace bullying by withdrawing socially at work, engaging in compulsive behaviors or ingesting substances that numb our pain, or even act out in ways that are aggressive or passive aggressive, becoming workplace bullies ourselves. In effect, workplace bullying significantly diminishes our ability to do our jobs.

In Jayda's story, I would argue that no one in Jayda's school, from the principal to Jayda's fellow teachers, had an authentic sense of inclusion safety. I think it's doubtful that the students in that school experienced a real sense of inclusion safety, given that the adults couldn't even provide it for one another. Jayda's colleagues had banned together in cliques in an effort to cement some sense of belonging and safety. However, these cliques attempted to exert power over one another, behaviors which were reinforced by the behaviors of the school administrator, who gave some groups undue influence. The teachers in Jayda's department perceived the success that Jayda had with her students as a threat to their own status, and they weaponized their biases against her.

Fortunately, some schools have taken action to prevent and address workplace bullying as part of their efforts to cultivate inclusion safety for all staff. I want to highlight the incredible transformation of one school that I worked with that found themselves stewing in a toxic workplace culture much like Jayda's school. After conducting a staff needs assessment similar to the one found in Chapter 2 of this book, much of the feedback (all of which was submitted anonymously) pointed to some troubling trends. Similar to Jayda's school, many staff reported feeling that the school was divided into social cliques and run by a small group of teachers who were the principal's favorites. Staff felt little trust among colleagues. Their responses detailed instances of workplace bullying, including gossip, backstabbing, and alleged instances where employees were encouraged to "spy on one another and report back to the administration."

When I presented the findings of the needs assessment to the school's leadership team, their initials responses were defensive and indignant. I was pretty sure that this would be our last coaching session. I honestly expected them to ask me to leave at any moment, especially when the principal broke down in tears. We decided to take a break to give everyone the opportunity to care for their own well-being, and when we returned, the principal shared from her heart in an expression of authenticity, vulnerability, and courage. She said that although the feedback was painful to hear, it was important and demanded a meaningful and significant response. So, we got to work designing an action plan.

My first suggestion, which I was shocked that they agreed to, was that we dismantle the current leadership team and restructure it. The first step in the process of building inclusion safety is creating a culture built upon representation and shared power. The new leadership team would have a representative from every grade level and department. Teachers voted to elect representatives from their respective grade or department team. The new team also included a paraprofessional, school psychologist, parent/family liaison, and office manager. We restructured the decision-making process to be consensus based rather than majority rules. This is a process we will explore further in the chapter on challenger safety. We also implemented a protocol for when the team had to make a decision that would affect the entire school community. In preparation for these decisions, members of the leadership team were tasked with gathering input from teachers, support staff (maintenance, food services, transportation, etc.), parents and caregivers, and students as needed.

Another important practice for cultivating inclusion safety was to establish a clear set of communication agreements for staff as well as protocols in place to maintain these agreements. These agreements were drafted, revised, and adopted in a process that involved input from the entire staff. Every team in the school began its meetings by reading aloud the communication agreements. And each team had a communication steward, a staff member whose sole responsibility was to ensure that the communication agreements were upheld and, if needed, intervene and redirect the conversation. We will explore communication agreements further in the chapter about contributor safety.

The school also developed a clear protocol to prevent and respond to workplace bullying. In the beginning of every school year, there is now a quick overview for the entire staff regarding workplace bullying, its forms, harmful effects, and steps to address it. These steps include first, being an upstander: If someone witnesses workplace bullying, they are encouraged to intervene. This can be as simple as saying, "This conversation doesn't feel appropriate for work," or, "When you say that about our colleague, it makes me feel uncomfortable. I'd appreciate if you spoke more respectfully about our coworkers." If the behavior persists, employees are to submit an anonymous complaint to the administration and/or Human Resources.

If someone is the target of workplace bullying, they are encouraged to speak up for themselves as soon as they experience the negative behavior *if* they feel safe enough to do so. This can be as simple as asking for the behavior to stop. However, depending upon the circumstances, directly addressing the bully may not be the best decision, which is why this choice is left up to the individual's discretion. If the problem persists, then employees are to submit a description of the behaviors, including an estimate of how long they have been going on, to their school administrator and/or Human Resources. Each reported case of workplace bullying is investigated by Human Resources, and an appropriate response is determined. The response may look like a restorative process in which the person who engaged in the workplace bullying is given the opportunity to stop the bullying behavior and take action to repair the relationships that have been harmed, or in more severe or persistent cases, the response may be more punitive, such as termination of employment. In the chapter on challenger safety, we will take a deeper dive into protocols as well as conflict resolution.

Last, and perhaps most important, the school staff engage in meaningful and fun opportunities to build and maintain positive relationships. Throughout the year, the staff has potlucks, celebrations, games, book clubs, exercise clubs, fantasy football leagues, morning coffee and tea, and a variety of other activities coordinated by the staff for staff. To deepen and strengthen relationships, staff are randomly assigned to discussion groups along with four to five other colleagues. Staff are randomly assigned to these groups because it gives them an opportunity to connect with colleagues who work in different grade levels and departments and to step outside of any cliques that may develop. The groups participate in "staff circles" or discussions that take place once a month during a staff meeting. Each discussion circle has a communication steward who facilitates the discussion using a talking piece that is passed to each member of the group to give an equal opportunity to participation. At each monthly discussion circle, all groups respond to the same one or two open-ended discussion questions. These questions invite educators to reflect both personally and professionally on an important topic or aspect of their work. One of the prompts given at the beginning of every school year is for each person to share with their colleagues what respect looks, sounds, and feels like for them. These staff circles create an opportunity for staff to know one another at a deeper level while reflecting upon their work as educators.

Developing and implementing all these practices took nearly 2 school years. We surveyed the staff prior to, during, and after the practices had been introduced and maintained. The results of these efforts were profoundly transformative. Staff reported a greater sense of belonging, improved communication and collaboration within their teams, and a sense that school leadership listened to and addressed their needs and concerns. This was a drastic improvement in the school's culture from when we started the journey. And it aligned with countless studies that have shown that when employees feel a sense of belonging at work, it improves morale, job satisfaction, retention rates, and job performance.

However, the most impressive results were reflected in student outcomes. We found that as inclusion safety increased, student outcomes significantly improved. We saw growth in mathematics and literacy scores, with many students making 2 years' worth of growth in a year's worth of time. Although surprising, these findings make perfect sense. *Inclusion safety is the foundation for collective efficacy.* When educators are included, not only in lip service but listened to, respected, and given meaningful opportunities to co-create a healthy school community, they are able to work together to meet the needs of their students. Each student becomes everyone's student.

School-Wide Inclusion Safety

Start	Stop	Continue
What could you & your colleagues start doing to create a more inclusive school?	*What should you & your colleagues stop doing because these behaviors exclude and harm others?*	*What practices should you & your colleagues continue doing to foster belonging & inclusion at school?*

REFLECTION QUESTIONS

1. Do you feel a sense of belonging at work? Why or why not?
2. Do you have any colleagues at work whom you feel superior to? Do you have any colleagues whom you feel inferior to? Do you treat these individuals differently?
3. What is one thing that you will do to help your colleagues feel more included at work?

KEY TAKEAWAYS

- Inclusion safety has a positive impact on educators' job satisfaction, retention, and performance.
- Shared identity and power shape the way that social groups are formed and maintained. Shared identity and power are complex. They can be maintained in ways that promote belonging and well-being or harm and exclusion.
- Identifying common goals, addressing feelings and needs, and finding ways to share power can help individuals and groups navigate challenges.
- When a school has a low level of inclusion safety, workplace bullying behaviors proliferate. Workplace bullying has a negative impact on educators' job performance and well-being.
- Ignoring workplace bullying will not make it go away. Take appropriate action to address it, and protect yourself and others.
- Excluding and harming others diminishes our own humanity. Inclusion safety is a moral imperative.
- Communication agreements, collaboration protocols, community-building activities, connected and firm leadership, and equity of voice in decision-making foster all four stages of psychological safety including inclusion safety.
- Inclusion safety is the foundation for collective efficacy.

PRACTICES, STRATEGIES, AND TOOLS

Individual Educator
• Introduce yourself to new staff members. • Make an effort to briefly and regularly interact with colleagues. • Learn and pronounce names correctly. • Focus on implementing evidence-based best practices to support the academic, behavioral, and social-emotional needs of students. Don't let divisive political discourse derail teaching and learning. • Be aware of your own biases, preferences, and prejudices. Make an effort to treat every staff member in a kind and professional manner.
Team
• Start meetings with a brief one-word check-in for team members to share how their day is going. • Acknowledge birthdays, anniversaries, and any major life events that team members choose to share with the team. • Uphold to communication agreements and protocols for effective collaboration. • Learn and pronounce names correctly. • Do not engage in or allow workplace bullying to persist among team members. Say something or seek help from the administration or Human Resources. • Ask each team member to share what respect looks and sounds like to them. Come up with a common definition of respect and what it looks and sounds like within your team. • Avoid comparison, criticism, and competition. Seek to understand, collaborate, and encourage. • Focus on implementing evidence-based best practices to support the academic, behavioral, and social-emotional needs of students. Don't let divisive political discourse derail teaching and learning. • Pause to allow think time during team discussions. • Share airtime. If you are someone who shares frequently, listen more. If you are typically quiet during meetings, share more often.
Administrator
• Provide professional development to all staff about workplace bullying and ways to address it. • Work with your staff to implement fun community-building activities throughout the school year. • Listen and respond to the feelings and needs of staff. Balance empathy with accountability. • Work with your staff to establish and maintain communication agreements for meetings and collaboration. • Learn and pronounce names correctly.

- Don't play favorites. Seek input from a diverse array of stakeholders including staff members you often disagree with or may not know well.
- Focus on implementing evidence-based best practices to support the academic, behavioral, and social-emotional needs of students. Don't let divisive political discourse derail teaching and learning.
- Be visible and present in your school. Brief, positive interactions make a big impact on peoples' sense of belonging at work.
- Learn more about cultural proficiency by reading books such as *Cultural Proficiency: A Manual for School Leaders* by Lindsey, Nuri-Robins, Terrell, and Lindsey.

5

LEARNER SAFETY

EDUCATOR LEARNING ACCELERATES STUDENT LEARNING

Educators don't need to be perfect to make a difference in the lives of their students. In fact, I don't believe that a "perfect" teacher exists, nor do I believe that a teacher can be a perfect fit for every one of their students. I believe in the power of the good enough teacher—the teacher who gets it right most of the time and occasionally misses the mark but responds with self-compassion, reflection, and a commitment to learn and do better. In my view, good teachers don't need to already know the answer to every question, the solution to every problem, or the strategy to meet every need. Instead, the most dynamic educators learn and grow right along with their students. These are the educators who treat the challenging behaviors, learning gaps, and unique needs of their students as invitations to expand their own ability to teach.

Teaching is a profession that demands tremendous agility. We are continually challenged to develop new mindsets and skills to meet the needs of the students in our classrooms, not the students we taught last year, or 10 years ago, or the students we wish we had, but the complex, evolving human beings sitting in our classrooms today. Their strengths and needs change day to day, and sometimes moment to moment, and the strategies that worked before may no longer be effective. Sometimes our students present needs so great that they demand that we improve our practice both individually and collectively. The needs of our students become a catalyst for our own professional learning and growth.

THE RISK IN LEARNING AND THE COST OF COMFORT

Learning is a risky endeavor for anyone but especially for teachers. We are often expected to have all the answers. It can feel like we get handed a new curriculum on a Friday, and by Monday we're getting observed and evaluated for our ability to teach it. There is often not much space, time, or grace afforded to teachers for their own learning. Not to mention, sometimes teachers make the worst students. I can certainly think of times I've walked into professional development assuming I already knew everything I needed to know and was too afraid to be honest about the things I needed to learn.

When I was a high school math teacher, our school had an influx of refugee students from multiple different countries. Not only did these students speak different languages, and have different degrees of exposure and proficiency with English, but they also had incredibly varied levels of knowledge and skills pertaining to mathematics. There were things I knew that I needed to improve on as their teacher. For example, I knew that I needed more strategies for teaching math to emerging language learners because my students were not making progress. Even though I knew I needed to improve my instruction, I did not take any action to learn about and implement new practices. I simply retaught the same lessons hoping that they would learn the content the second time around, which they did not.

There were also things that I could have done to better to support my students that I was completely unaware of at the time. For example, at that time there was no mainstream awareness of the impact of trauma on learning. I had no idea that there were teaching practices I could implement to better address the social-emotional, behavioral, and cognitive needs of these young people who had experienced significant trauma as refugees. I don't blame myself for not knowing what I didn't know. However, I regret not making the effort to seek out additional resources. My students were struggling, but I was too proud to admit that my best wasn't good enough. I wasn't brave enough to ask for feedback, guidance, and support. I was worried that if I admitted to my administrator and colleagues that I needed help, they'd think less of me. Instead, I played it safe by continuing to teach the same way I always had, and my students did not get the support that they needed.

Timothy R. Clark has said that when you embark on a learning journey, "You naturally look around and do a risk/reward calculation in your head: 'If I ask that question, or request help, or make a suggestion, or admit I don't know, or make a mistake, what will it cost me? Can I be myself? Will I look stupid? Am I on trial? Will people laugh? Will they ignore me? Will I hurt my prospects? Will I damage my reputation?' In every learning context, consciously or not, we assess the level of interpersonal risk around us."[1] If the interpersonal risk is too great, then it can prevent any learning from taking place. Teachers may face barriers to learning that are interpersonal, structural, or even intrapersonal. At times our greatest resistance to learning can come from within.

As teachers we have a professional duty to continue to learn throughout our careers. Thankfully, we will explore ways that educators have cultivated learner safety for themselves, their teams, and their schools. Learner safety is the encouragement, opportunity, and support necessary for learning. Learner safety is rooted in a deep respect for each person's need to learn and grow. Continuing to learn gives our careers vitality and relevance and ensures that our students receive evidence-based instruction that builds the skills they'll need to navigate a rapidly changing, and increasingly complex, world.

REFLECTION QUESTIONS

1. Do you feel comfortable asking for feedback, guidance, or support in your school? Why or why not?
2. Have you ever felt pressured to be the "perfect educator" who has all the answers and a solution for every problem? If so, how has this affected you?

COMPETITION VERSUS COLLABORATION

In Chapter 1, we met Kurt, a first-year high school social studies teacher who was struggling to learn the ropes in a school that provided little support to new teachers. The expectations placed on Kurt and his colleagues were high. Kurt's school was the highest-performing high school in his town and one of the highest performing in the state. Teachers at Kurt's school had their days scheduled down to the minute. Sometimes teachers felt like they spent more time in meetings talking about teaching than they did teaching. Teachers met in professional learning communities, department meetings, grade-level meetings, student support team meetings, common planning meetings with special education staff, and committee meetings. They also had monthly data nights when teachers worked an additional 3 hours after the school day ended analyzing data and developing action plans to support struggling students. You would think that with all these meetings, there would be a high degree of collaboration among the staff. However, that was not the case at this school.

Kurt's school culture could best be characterized as competitive rather than collaborative. During meetings, teachers were cautious about what they chose to share. Teachers found it safer to share examples of growth rather than discuss challenges. As a result, the meetings typically focused on the teachers (often the same ones from week to week) who were having the greatest success with their students. These teachers would talk about instructional moves they were doing in their classrooms. Meanwhile, everyone else would sort of keep their head down, pore over their own assessment data, and hope to avoid the spotlight while they anxiously tried to figure out how to teach their students who weren't making progress. These meetings seemed to be as much about highlighting what was working as shaming the other teachers for not producing similar results. Teachers didn't feel safe enough to discuss challenges because there was the risk of being viewed by their colleagues as inferior or incompetent. If a teacher was brave enough to discuss a challenge they were facing in the classroom and ask for input or assistance, their colleagues typically responded with scrutiny rather than support.

Kurt learned this lesson the hard way. During a department meeting, he expressed concern about the performance of several of his students on the document-based essay of their midterm exam. He spoke about how his students had failed to develop logical thesis statements, craft coherent arguments, or accurately cite sources. He was overwhelmed by the gaps in his students' writing abilities and didn't know where to begin. "I taught all of this," he said exasperated. "We practiced it together. We went through the entire process from outlining to revising. We analyzed sample essays. I gave them graphic organizers. They wrote practice essays, and then I sat with them, and we evaluated their writing together with a rubric. And they still aren't getting it. Some of them can't even write an intro paragraph that makes sense. What should I do?"

The room was silent after Kurt finished speaking. Kurt noticed as Mrs. Francis, one of the other social studies teachers, made eye contact with a colleague, then smirked and shook her head disapprovingly. To which the colleague reacted by stifling a laugh. Another teacher on the team chimed in, "I have two concerns about what you shared Kurt. When you did all those things with your students, were they quiet and focused? Or were you allowing them to get away with goofing off and being off task? My other concern is about pacing because everything you mentioned takes a lot of time, and it's important that we keep moving through the curriculum." After this was said, Kurt's cheeks flushed, and his throat tightened. He felt a mix of humiliation, hurt, and defensive anger. He didn't know how to respond and never got the opportunity to. The department chair spoke next, bringing the meeting to a close with, "We will follow up on this, Kurt. Thank you for bringing it to our attention."

The following day, the principal visited Kurt's third-period class unannounced. He sat in the back of the room taking notes for the entire period. During his lunch, Kurt got an email from the principal requesting a meeting the next day. He asked Kurt to the bring the lesson plan for the class period that was observed. Kurt hardly slept that night. He kept replaying the class observation in his head. He was anticipating every critique and trying to think of a way to defend himself. The next day, with his stomach in knots and his lesson plan in hand, Kurt went to his principal's office. The principal was seated at his desk with Kurt's electronic gradebook pulled on his computer. What followed was an excruciating 45 minutes during which Kurt had to go over his lesson plan, share what he felt his strengths and growth areas were as a teacher, and discuss his students' performance on their midterm exam.

At the end of the meeting, the principal said, "For the next 4 weeks, I'd like you to spend second period each Monday in Mrs. Francis's class. She's our highest-performing social studies teacher, and I think you can learn a lot from observing her in action. I know you typically have common planning during that period, but this would be a better use of your time." Kurt thanked his principal and left the meeting with a headache, sweat stains on his shirt, and a deep, sinking feeling in his stomach. In a different school, Mrs. Francis might decide to mentor Kurt as a new teacher and take him under her wing. Kurt might even be given the opportunity to meet with a special education teacher who could offer Kurt some suggestions, or assistance, to better support struggling writers. These are some of the things that might happen in a school with a higher degree of learner safety. However, that wasn't Kurt's school.

The following Monday, Kurt showed up to Mrs. Francis's second-period class. Upon entering the room, he could hear students whisper to one another about his unexpected appearance in their class. Mrs. Francis announced that Kurt would be visiting each Monday for the next month to learn ways to improve his instruction. She pointed to an empty seat in the back of the classroom. He could hear students making jokes about him being in trouble. He sat in the back of the class and began taking notes. He wasn't sure what he was supposed to be taking notes on, but he knew that his principal would likely want to know what he had learned from this experience.

Kurt had to admit that Mrs. Francis was an impressive teacher. Her class was highly structured, students were focused and engaged, and the lesson seemed to flow seamlessly. However, watching her each week felt like trying a new fancy dessert. The dessert was amazing, but he never learned anything about the ingredients that went into it or what it took to bake it. Mrs. Francis chose not to share with Kurt about the hours she devoted to analyzing student work, tailoring her instruction, and helping her students learn how to assess their own progress, not to mention, the time spent developing, modeling, and practicing routines with her students so that in every minute of each period, her students knew what was expected and how to engage.

Mrs. Francis had spent years refining her skills as a teacher, and she didn't have any intention of sharing her hard-earned knowledge with Kurt or any other teacher. She had made considerable sacrifices in her devotion to her job. She worked at school until 8 pm almost every weeknight. She came in on weekends to prepare for the week ahead. She chaired committees. She taught after-school tutoring. She bent over backward to help students learn. She didn't kiss ass like some of her colleagues did to win favor. Instead, she let the impact of her efforts, as evidenced by the success of her students, speak for itself. When the principal told her that Kurt would be observing her, it felt like an acknowledgment of her hard work, but it also seemed to reinforce a perception she had that the school, and the district, were a sort of boys' club. She had never seen a female teacher struggle and get additional support from the administration. In fact, quite the opposite, she had watched female colleagues get written up and evaluated so harshly that they resigned. Certainly, no one helped her get to where she was in her career, and in her opinion, that made her a better teacher. The thought of having to mentor Kurt, on top of her already busy schedule, seemed like an undue burden. She had too many students who needed her, and he was an adult. If Kurt couldn't pull his own weight, then he needed to move on.

As for Kurt, observing Mrs. Francis sparked envy and considerable self-criticism. He wished that his students responded to him with the same disciplined focus that Mrs. Francis evoked in her students. However, those 4 weeks observing her class provided him with little insight into how he could get from where he was as a teacher to where he wanted to be. The one thing he did learn from the experience was never to ask for help during a meeting again.

REFLECTION QUESTIONS

1. What were some of the interpersonal behaviors and dynamics that robbed Kurt of an experience of learner safety? Do any of these behaviors and dynamics exist within your school?
2. To what extent are teachers within your school provided the resources (e.g., professional development, time to collaborate, coaching, etc.) that they need to learn and grow professionally?

I had the opportunity to visit Kurt's school and observed that there was one department that had more learner safety than any other. The English department was defined by cooperation and collaboration rather than competition. I sat in on a department meeting, expecting the same quiet tension that I experienced in the other meetings. Instead, there was authentic sharing, empathy, vulnerability, and a felt sense of that they had one another's back. Teachers brought up challenges, and colleagues offered suggestions and support rather than judgment. At one point a teacher mentioned a student who had become despondent and disengaged, and a colleague chimed in, "I taught him last year. He can be tough, but we had a good relationship. If it would help, I can talk with him and see what's going," to which the teacher expressed appreciation.

I told them that their department meeting was a breath of fresh air. It was great to see educators in their school helping one another. Even though the administration and their colleagues had established a culture of competition and relentless perfectionism, these teachers acted within their sphere of influence to create something better. One of the teachers responded, "We do things differently. This is a tough building; we know that we need each other. I've heard from friends in other departments that if a teacher's students aren't performing at standard, or above, then that teacher is viewed as the weakest link, the one dragging down the rest of their department. And that mentality influences how we treat the kids."

I asked the teacher to elaborate, and she said, "Listen to the way some teachers here talk about students and their families. Especially if those students are English learners (ELs), or they have an IEP, a lot of teachers don't want to teach them. Those kids get pushed off on the teacher with the lowest rank in their department. And, if it weren't for our school counselor and our special ed and language teachers, then those students would have no one to advocate for them." This made me think about Kurt, who despite being a first-year teacher, had the highest number of ELs and students with disabilities in his department. The teacher with the least amount of experience was given the students with the greatest needs. In a school that lacks learner safety, this makes sense. Teaching a student with significant cognitive and/or linguistic needs means that the teacher will also need to learn. The teacher will have to try new strategies, develop new skills, and grow in ways that will likely be uncomfortable and put them at risk for being judged by their colleagues and their administration if their students don't excel. It's not surprising then that teachers would pull rank and try to get as many academically proficient students as possible to stack the deck in their favor. The unfortunate reality, though, is that then the students don't receive the support they need.

"We look at it differently," another teacher in the department went on to say. "The students with the greatest needs are the ones who need us the most. And its humbling. If I get a tough group of students this year, then my team will rally around me. They'll brainstorm strategies right along with me because next year one of them could be in my position. We look for ways to help each other out." Their humility to admit when they don't have the answer to a problem, and their willingness to collaboratively find a solution, are hallmarks of learner safety.

One teacher went on, "This might sound crazy, but one of our favorite things to discuss are the lessons that totally bomb, the ones where the kids walk away totally confused or having learned nothing. We learn so much as a team from dissecting those kinds of lessons to figure out where we went wrong and what we could do differently." This process of framing mistakes as learning opportunities was a stark contrast from Kurt's team, which seemed to make space only for perfect. These teachers also undoubtedly gained considerable insight from reflecting on these lessons. As Timothy R. Clark has said,

"Indeed, if you're really trying, there should be no stigma, no shame, and no embarrassment associated with failure. It's simply a steppingstone. We should reward failure because it's not failure; it's progress. The examination of failure is often more beneficial that the examination of success."[2]

Finally, I asked the team if they experienced any negativity from other professionals in the building for doing things differently. One of the teachers responded, "Absolutely. They're probably jealous because we're a refuge for one another. But we chose to be that as a team rather than going along with the status quo. We said we aren't going to pretend to be perfect. We are gonna be messy and powerful. I don't think I could work at this school if I was in another department. I need *this* team. And the most important thing is that our students make progress, so at the end of the day, everyone else lets us do our thing because it's working." What this teacher described as "messy" was a willingness to confront challenges head-on. If a student, or group of students, wasn't making progress, they looked for ways to address the problem. In that process, there may be venting, tears, or laughter, but ultimately the team moved toward improving their practice while staying mindful of their impact.

This team's ability to step into the gap, with all the uncertainty, frustration, and overwhelm that comes with it, and take action made them powerful. They named the learning needs of their students, admitted when they didn't know what else to do, and then did the work together (which sometimes involved research, strategy, innovation) until they determined the next right step. Then they implemented new practices, assessed their impact, and were brave enough to own the results of their efforts without shame or blame. Yes, they celebrated student progress, but the real victory for them was that they didn't give up; they stayed in the productive struggle of learning and growth. This is learner safety in the truest sense.

REFLECTION QUESTIONS

1. What has been one of your most meaningful learning experiences as an educator?
2. Has there been a time where you had to adapt and try something different to meet the needs of a student? What was that experience like for you? How did you know if what you did made a difference?

PUTTING OUT FIRES ALL DAY EVERY DAY

At Joyce Elementary, all students qualified for free or reduced lunch. In fact, school was the place where many of them ate their meals for the day. Students' parents and caregivers struggled to find work that paid a living wage. Many of these families had experienced housing insecurity, food instability, and community violence. Several students arrived at school each day with their nervous systems dysregulated by the chronic stress of poverty, hunger, inequity, and trauma.

I was working as a coach with this school, supporting them in developing and implementing trauma-informed social-emotional and behavioral supports. I spent my first couple days with them observing the day-to-day operations of the school. I watched as the school administrators and support staff spent the day putting out fires, chasing students who eloped from class, having heart-to-hearts with crying kids, trying to de-escalate screaming students, breaking up fights, and clearing students from classrooms while another student hurled obscenities and chairs at them.

Meanwhile, the line of students waiting outside the principal's office grew steadily throughout the day. Students sent there due to less severe, although still challenging, misbehaviors enjoyed talking and laughing with each other as the office manager attempted in vain to have them wait quietly. Around the corner from the front office, the school nurse's office was overflowing as usual with students complaining of headaches, stomachaches, and maladies, many of which seemed to remarkably disappear when it was time for that student's class to get lunch or go to recess. I don't think I ever saw the school's counselor sit down, let alone check her email, eat lunch, or run a counseling group. Her job seemed to resemble a school dean more than a counselor, given how much of the day she spent responding to behavioral escalations. All this would be going on as the number of students roaming the halls and congregating near the bathrooms increased with each passing hour.

Teachers spent the entire day constantly redirecting and reacting to behaviors. Time and again, I would a witness a teacher become as dysregulated as the students. Then a power struggle would ensue that usually resulted in the teacher calling the office for assistance. The power struggle would crescendo to a full-on shouting match by the time an administrator, or member of the support staff, arrived to escort the student out of class. Then an hour later, the same student would get brought back to the classroom with a smile on their face like they'd just gone to Disneyland. The student would reenter the room, wait until the adult who brought them had left, and start acting up again. Meanwhile, from the teacher's perspective, the student was rewarded for their misbehavior by getting a break from the class.

On a few occasions, I watched students hit and kick teachers during escalations, only to be brought back later that day to say, "I'm sorry," before going on to further disrupt the class with more off-task behavior. In situations like this, the teacher would typically give up. There was no point in attempting to redirect the child's behavior when all their previous efforts had gotten them was a bruised shin. There was also no follow-up to develop a plan to better support the teacher and the student. Most of the teachers I spoke to described being in "survival mode," trying to make it through each workday. Some staff said that it felt like the kids were running the school. However, the sad reality is that the students were crying for help through their behavior. They needed structure and connection. This was a school run by collective trauma.

Teachers were pushed past their limits and exhausted from responding to challenging behaviors all day long. They found it impossible to teach. From their perspective, students weren't held accountable for misbehavior, and as a result, those behaviors worsened and disrupted learning. Some of the teachers who had been at the school for several years waxed nostalgic about better days back when the school had a different principal who didn't tolerate students' misbehavior. According to them, the students used to be more respectful, the parents were more involved, and the teachers held more authority. Whether or not these recollections were accurate, they conveyed a sentiment held by the many teachers that the current state of affairs wasn't working for anyone. Evidence of this could be seen in the fact that most students finished fifth grade at Joyce Elementary with a third grade reading level as well as significant gaps in their conceptual and procedural understanding of mathematics.

What concerned me most was seeing everyone react to the same types of behaviors every day; yet there was no time devoted to developing and implementing proactive and responsive school-wide practices to address students' social-emotional and behavioral needs. In other words, there was no time spent developing effective systems. Each teacher's classroom was its own island. The teacher closed their classroom door after the morning bell and did their best to survive the day. Many were thankful to make it to the end of the school day and be one step closer to summer break. Some teachers were still motivated to try new things, whether out of hope or desperation: They'd search online and in books for new strategies to try. They'd implement a new practice hoping this would be the solution to their problem. Then a few days or a couple weeks later, they'd abandon it in hopes of finding something better.

I have taught in and coached schools like this one. I have also witnessed schools like this undergo dramatic transformations but never because of a single strategy. Strategies don't transform schools; effective systems do. Systems require teams, teamwork, and evidence of impact. Effective systems are driven by educators who have the encouragement, structure, and support that facilitate growth; in other words, effective systems require learner safety. After all, student outcomes improve when educators' mindsets and practices improve. Professional learning is nearly impossible to initiate and sustain when the majority of staff feel overwhelmed, demoralized, defeated, unsupported, and isolated.

My first professional development session with the staff was painful. The burnout and despair in the room was palpable. Many of the educators were on their cell phones or browsing the internet on their laptops while I spoke. Whenever I asked a question, there would be a long silence until someone begrudgingly raised a hand to respond. I couldn't blame them. Their disengagement seemed like presenteeism, a symptom of burnout. Presenteeism is when professionals are physically present at work but are not fully engaged. It's a way to conserve as much as energy as you can while staying in a job that drains you. Not to mention, they'd probably sat through dozens of professional development sessions prior to this one that were either irrelevant to their needs or ineffectual at producing real change.

THE SEDUCTIVE TRAP OF BLAME

The only topic that seemed to enliven them was talking about how bad things were. Everyone was quick to chime in about the horrible state of their school. The long list of problems was accompanied by a litany of blame: the students were disrespectful, the parents didn't care, the administration was too permissive, and so on. Social scientists such as Brené Brown have found that expressing blame releases emotional pain and discomfort. This research has also shown that as blame increases, our sense of responsibility and empathy decrease.[3] Blame becomes a seductive trap. In the short term, it allows us to vent our anger, pain, and frustration, but it leaves us disempowered to do anything about their root causes.

Any time I suggested a potential step toward addressing a problem, I'd see eyes glaze over with resignation and cynicism. "That will never work" started to feel like a choral response anytime I so much as hinted at doing things differently. I'll be honest, as a coach, even I wanted to give up. I had to remind myself that at the heart of all this despair, resignation, and blame was a fixed mindset. This staff had come to believe that this was simply the way things were and there was nothing they could do to change it. But how can you encourage a growth mindset when people are exhausted, stewing in blame, stuck in the past, looking for things to fail, or in other words, manifesting the symptoms of burnout caused from working in a dysfunctional system?

After all, our mindsets as educators have a significant impact on student outcomes. Research has shown that educators' self-efficacy beliefs affect student achievement.[4] In fact, these beliefs can become self-fulfilling prophecies. For example, if a teacher believes they can positively affect student academic achievement, then their students are more likely make progress. However, let's say a teacher has a student who misbehaves on the first day of school, and the teacher thinks, "Well, I got a bad one. Nothing I can do about it." That student will likely spend a good amount of the year in the principal's office. Shifting our mindset can be harder, though, than we might expect. It's not simply a matter of positive thinking; at some point it needs to be supported by evidence of impact.

Why would educators risk learning and implementing new practices when there is no guarantee of success? Let's be honest; change is difficult. Learning and developing new skills requires time, energy, focus, and perseverance. And, as human beings we are wired, especially when we're under chronic stress, to do what is the most familiar to us, in other words, to stay the same. We would rather remain in our comfort zone and avoid the pain required to grow, that is, unless our comfort zone is on fire. And that was the catalyst that sparked a transformative learning journey at Joyce Elementary, not a literal fire but the moment that one grade-level team made the decision that staying the same was more painful than risking change.

MINDSET MATTERS

After one of our staff professional development sessions, the fourth grade teachers came to talk to me. They asked if I'd be willing to coach their team on implementing the practices that I talked about that day. I was thrilled at the prospect. Then I realized that these teachers, whether they intended to or not, had figured out how to shift the mindset of their staff toward learning and professional growth. As human beings we are more likely to change our behavior when we believe that behavior will result in a favorable outcome. So, at first, we act from some degree of hope, and then that hope becomes certainty when we see results. However, hope at Joyce Elementary was in short supply.

Thankfully, research on educator self and collective efficacy tells us that vicarious experiences of success can inspire hope and encourage growth, meaning that educators are more likely to become motivated to improve their practice when they hear a colleague share about something they've done that worked in their classroom.[5] This makes sense because that colleague teaches the same population of students, works in the same school, and is, therefore, a more reliable source of information than any outsider. If this fourth grade team could implement new practices and share their journey with the rest of the staff, it would have potential to shift mindsets and spark systemic change.

We got right to work meeting each week for coaching sessions. We started by building a strong foundation in the fourth grade classrooms grounded in routines, relationships, and regulation. Over time, we implemented clearer expectations, consistent routines, redirection practices rooted in connection, a consequencing protocol informed by restorative practices and conducted a relationship inventory, strengthened bonds with students who had low levels of belonging, and made time and space for regulation practices throughout the school day. As a result, we saw a significant decrease in challenging behaviors and an increase in prosocial behaviors. Teachers also shared anecdotal data about a perceived improvement in overall student mood and well-being.

The teachers decided that each time we met, each member of their team would share a rose, thorn, and bud. The rose was a positive impact the teacher saw as a result of implementing one of the new practices. The thorn was a challenge that the teacher wanted assistance addressing. We wrote down these challenges and spent time discussing each one, coming up with ideas or plans to address it. We closed each session by sharing a bud, which was one thing each teacher was taking away from that day's discussion that inspired hope or action. The buds were often potential solutions to thorns. This rose, thorn, and bud structure nurtured a sense of learner safety among the team by creating a simple way to share about strengths and challenges and come up with new ideas.

Each month during the whole-staff professional development session, the fourth grade team shared about one of the new practices that they had implemented in their classrooms. They helped their colleagues understand why it was important, how they implemented and refined it, and how they assessed whether it was working. This also helped them see why it was better than what they had done in the past. They shared challenges and successes, making it clear that their efforts were a work in progress. These teachers modeled for their colleagues that it was OK to start somewhere and improve as you go. I watched as the mindset of their colleagues shifted, and they engaged in a collective learning process. Teachers asked questions, proposed potential obstacles, and expressed genuine interest in applying what they were learning in their own classrooms. The staff ultimately identified five practices that they wanted to focus on implementing school-wide: welcoming routines and optimistic closures, regulation activities, relationship inventories, and the consequencing protocol. The following year, we focused on implementing these practices throughout this school, laying a foundation upon which we built additional supports and interventions.

None of this would have been possible had it not been for that fourth grade team. Joyce Elementary's journey offers some important insight into the power of starting small, piloting new methods, sharing vicarious experiences of success, and inviting staff to decide upon their collective learning journey. This helps us see how the learner safety we cultivate within our grade-level and/or department teams can have a ripple effect that benefits the entire school.

REFLECTION QUESTIONS

1. Does blame show up in the conversations that educators have in your school? If so, how?
2. Can you think of a time when your mindset shifted from a fixed to a growth mindset? What caused that shift for you?

INITIATIVE FATIGUE

Initiative fatigue is the enemy of learner safety—one that is often hard for teachers to address on their own because it's typically a top-down problem. Federal, state, and district mandates can require schools to implement multiple new initiatives, programs, and curricula at the same time. When this happens, educators are spread so thin that it compromises their efficacy and the fidelity with which they can implement these new initiatives. The result is that educators are forced to cut corners and check boxes to comply with all that is expected of them. They become busy doing all the things that are expected of them without knowing if any of these things are working. Real professional learning and growth can be hijacked by a culture of compliance. Or, as one teacher whose school had implemented 11 new programs in 3 years, said to me rather bluntly, "I do what I'm told to cover my ass."

Brooks Middle School was deep in initiative fatigue. Over the course of 2 years, the district had introduced: new ELA and mathematics curricula; a teacher evaluation system; a social-emotional learning (SEL) curriculum; an equity, inclusion, and culturally responsive teaching initiative; and a multi-tiered positive behavior program. The school had also brought me in as a coach to support the integration of trauma-informed practices. In addition, the teachers were receiving professional development trainings on project-based learning and STEM integration across content areas. Teachers were working tirelessly to keep up with all that was being asked of them.

However, there were so many new programs, curricula, and initiatives that it felt impossible for teachers to achieve proficiency in any one of them. All these changes demanded considerable time to organize, plan, and prepare. District administrators from the Curriculum, Instruction, and Assessment Department had started observing teachers almost immediately after the new English language arts and mathematics curricula were introduced. Teachers had almost no time to familiarize themselves with the new content and felt like they were learning it right along with the students. Meanwhile, another group of district administrators from the Department of Diversity, Equity, and Inclusion had also started observing teachers on their culturally responsive teaching practices. Teachers were getting contradictory feedback from the two different groups of administrators. On the one hand, they were told to implement the new English language arts and math curricula with absolute fidelity, even though neither of these curricula reflected or engaged the cultures and identities of their students. On the other hand, they were told to modify the curricula and go beyond what they were given to teach to more authentically engage the perspectives and lived experiences of their students. The conflicting messaging resulted in teachers feeling like they needed to put on a different show depending upon who came into their classroom to observe.

The lack of alignment and integration of initiatives at the district level had significantly hindered teachers' opportunities to learn and grow. When multiple initiatives are introduced, they inevitably compete for resources, especially the already scarce resource of time: time for teachers to learn new content and skills, planning time, time during the school day for implementation in the classroom, and time for progress monitoring and refinement. When multiple initiatives are introduced in ways that are poorly aligned and integrated, then the teachers' learning journey is doomed to be superficial at best, which creates yet another obstacle to their success in the classroom.

In the midst of all this change and challenge, a group of teachers from Brooks Middle School attended a multiday certification program in restorative practices. They came back to school inspired by all that they had learned and immediately scheduled a meeting with their principal. They shared with their principal about the ways the restorative practices would build community, promote positive behavior, foster accountability, and deepen learning. Although the principal appreciated their enthusiasm and agreed with what they shared, she was also keenly aware that most of her staff was overwhelmed by initiative fatigue. The last thing they wanted was one more thing added to their already full plates.

She told the teachers that they could certainly implement some of these practices in their own classrooms, but she felt that the rest of the staff were not ready. The teachers begged to differ. They felt that there was a way that restorative practices could be aligned and integrated that would be efficient and support many of the new initiatives. In fact, it could potentially lessen teachers' workload. This piqued the principal's interest. The teachers explained that the initial focus for implementing restorative practices would be class circles. If they could focus on circles as a foundation, then in future years they could build upon that to include restorative dialogue and conferences to address conflict and repair harm as needed. Every teacher in the school taught an advisory period during which they delivered lessons from the SEL curriculum. Teachers had complained about the SEL curriculum because students didn't find it relevant.

This group of teachers proposed to their principal that they would take the topics of the SEL curriculum and create a set of discussion questions that the rest of the teachers could use during circles in daily advisory. After all, social-emotional learning is most impactful when students are given opportunities to *practice* social and emotional skills. The current SEL curriculum was mostly "sit and get." Circles, however, would give students the opportunity to practice communication skills by considering multiple perspectives, managing emotions and impulses, building relationships, and decision-making. Circle questions could also invite students to share about their perspectives and lived experiences, making them culturally responsive. Teachers were also given the choice to integrate circles beyond advisory to discuss academic topics in their other classes.

THE POWER OF DE-IMPLEMENTATION

The principal appreciated that the teachers had come up with thoughtful ways to align and integrate circles with the other programs, initiatives, and goals of the school and district. Some of their suggestions would also create space for teachers to implement circles by *de-implementing* aspects of the SEL curriculum. De-implementation is a process best delineated by educator, school coach, and author Peter Dewitt in his book *De-Implementation: Creating the Space to Focus on What Works*. According to DeWitt, de-implementation involves identifying low-value practices that are ineffective, cause harm, and/or are no longer needed and gradually reducing or eliminating them.[6] De-implementation creates space for educators to implement more impactful practices while reducing initiative fatigue and burnout.

In this instance, teachers would still use topics from the SEL curriculum, but they would no longer teach lessons directly from it. Instead, they'd embed these topics within circles using discussion questions that were more engaging and culturally responsive. Because this team of teachers had offered to develop the questions for each advisory circle, this would also free up planning time for teachers that was previously spent focused on the SEL curriculum. The principal thought that the rest of the staff would appreciate this, but she still wanted to give them an opportunity to weigh in before any decisions were made. She offered to give this group time during the next staff in-service day to share about restorative practices and to ask the staff if circles was something the other teachers wanted to take on.

After their presentation, teachers overwhelmingly agreed that circles were the next right step for their school. They also proposed that circles could be used to give students the opportunity to discuss ways to prevent and address school-wide behavioral and social-emotional challenges. This would give students a voice in shaping the issues that directly affected them, their safety, and their learning, which felt more developmentally appropriate for early adolescents than the current behavior program, which relied heavily on points and rewards. Teachers felt like this system wasn't having an impact on student behavior. Most students didn't seem to care about the points system. The teachers proposed a further step in the de-implementation process. If they were able to use circles in ways that produced a measurable improvement in student behavior (e.g., a reduction in referrals, etc.), then they wanted to gradually de-implement the points system of the current behavior program. The principal knew that this would likely get pushback from the district, but it was a battle she was willing to fight *if* it would benefit her staff *and* the circles proved to be more effective than the current behavior program's points system in managing student behavior.

COLLECTIVE CARE BEFORE CHANGE

The principal then did something that I found remarkable. She asked the staff to complete a brief, six-question, multiple-choice, well-being survey, adapted from the ProQOL[7] and the work of Dr. Bryan Sexton and his colleagues, who research workplace resilience and well-being.[8]

STAFF WELL-BEING SURVEY

Think about work within the last 30 days, and respond to each question on a scale from Never, Rarely, Sometimes, Often to Almost Always.

1. I feel satisfaction from doing my job.
2. I feel connected to the people I work with.
3. I feel inspired by my work.
4. I skip meals during the workday because I am so busy.
5. I don't get adequate sleep because of work.
6. I change or cancel plans with family and/or friends due to my work schedule.

This anonymous online survey took about 3 minutes for the entire staff to complete. The results showed that majority of the staff felt satisfaction, connection, and inspiration often or almost always. These were positive findings. However, the results also showed that nearly 80% of the staff reported skipping meals, not getting enough sleep, and changing or canceling plans because of work. These findings indicated that the majority of staff were showing the early signs of burnout. If this trend persisted then over time, those experiences of satisfaction, connection, and inspiration would likely diminish.

The principal said to her staff, "One of my commitments as a principal is to take care of you, so you can take care of our students." She explained that despite their initial enthusiasm, circles can be difficult to facilitate. They require considerable time, effort, skill, creativity, and reflection because students often struggle, especially in the beginning, to participate in them appropriately, respectfully, and authentically. To ensure this learning journey would be successful she wanted to make sure that staff had the capacity for it. This six-question survey showed that things needed to be done to build that capacity. She then asked the staff to come up with a list of ways they could care for themselves and one another. The teachers spent time brainstorming and came up with three action steps: stop sending and/or responding to work text messages and emails during the weekend (unless it is truly an urgent matter or emergency); take your lunch and don't feel guilty about it; and use funds from the school's social committee to create a staff mindfulness room. I thought this move by the principal was incredibly wise and compassionate. I can't count how many worthy initiatives I have seen fail simply because teachers were overwhelmed, exhausted, or suffering from burnout.

CELEBRATING SMALL WINS

The next step in the process involved structuring the learning process in ways that would sustain engagement and participation while facilitating teachers' acquisition of knowledge and skills. To do this, teachers knew that they needed to pace the learning process in a way that was manageable. Introducing a new program and expecting educators to implement it flawlessly the next day is unrealistic, demoralizing, and all too common. Instead, they divided the learning journey into phases with clear observable goals or what they called "small wins." These small wins included: students being able to get themselves and their desks into and out of circle formation quickly, quietly, and safely; completing a welcoming routine at the start of a circle including a mindfulness activity and brief check-in; completing one round of discussion using a discussion question or prompt and moving to additional rounds as needed; and ending the circle with a closing routine. They also asked teachers to look for other qualitative aspects of improvement such as the percentage of students who participate in the discussion; creative modifications that remove barriers to participation; and the depth with which students' share. They also identified student outcomes that they would monitor along the way, including behavior data as well as a students' responses to a belongingness survey.

The team's decision to identify these small wins was incredibly smart. We know that to facilitate and sustain motivation during the learning process, people need to see signs of progress. When new programs and curricula are introduced, teachers are often told that it will take years to see results. For systemic change within their school, they are typically told to wait anywhere from 3 to 7 years. Imagine telling people that if they went on a diet and started exercising, they might lose weight in 3 years. Few people would likely stick with a behavior change that long without some sign of progress. Teachers are no different. In fact, according to Jim Knight's work on instructional coaching and teacher efficacy, educators need to see results in weeks and not several months or years.[9] By breaking down the circle implementation process into small wins, educators could assess their progress and pinpoint areas where they were stuck.

During the professional development journey that followed, the guiding teachers acted as peer mentors. These peer mentors made themselves available to model, co-facilitate, and observe other teachers' circles to provide helpful feedback. The peer mentors and their colleagues developed a list of agreements for giving and receiving constructive feedback. Quality feedback is critical to learning. The staff agreed that when giving constructive feedback, the feedback needed to be specific, timely, goal oriented, encouraging, and actionable. They also agreed that when receiving feedback, they would ask clarifying questions, maintain a growth mindset, and be willing to act on the feedback. To further aid the learning process, the peer mentors invited their colleagues to submit anonymous questions and challenges pertaining to class circles. They made time during staff meetings to share successes and problem-solve challenges. This allowed the staff to learn together in a way that encouraged vulnerability, creativity, and collaboration.

This story of Brooks Middle School focuses on circles; however, it highlights moves that can cultivate learner safety in any professional growth journey. The administrator listened to and cared for her staff. Educators co-created a learning goal for their school. They reflected on their own well-being and found ways to practice self and collective care throughout the learning process. Space was created for the learning journey through de-implementation. Teachers developed efficient and purposeful ways to align and integrate multiple initiatives. They designed the learning process so that colleagues would be able to monitor progress and celebrate small wins. Along the way, there were opportunities to share successes, ask questions, discuss challenges, and receive helpful feedback and support. Overall, this process cultivated and sustained learner safety in the face of initiative fatigue and burnout.

WHAT WE'VE LEARNED SO FAR

The case studies that we've explored in this chapter provide insight into barriers to learner safety, including overly competitive environments, perfectionism, fixed mindsets, burnout, and initiative fatigue. They also show us how educators overcame these barriers: educators who found ways to encourage professional learning and structured the learning process in ways that sustained productive struggle. We saw how they reduced interpersonal risk though vulnerability and mutual support. They were brave enough to push back against the stifling pressure of perfect and allow themselves to be "messy and powerful."

They structured the learning process in ways that encouraged participation and honored the learning needs of educators. They did this through piloting new strategies, sharing vicarious experiences of success, collaborative problem-solving, teacher-to-teacher collaboration, and celebrating small wins. In the example of Brooks Middle School, we saw an administrator whose humility and care facilitated her staff's professional growth. She listened to her teachers and honored their needs in ways that aligned with the priorities of the school. When administrators and teachers work together to cultivate learner safety, the results can dramatically shift a school's culture and outcomes.

REFLECTION QUESTIONS

1. What risks and/or barriers to professional learning have you encountered?
2. What helps you learn and grow as an educator? What can you do to assist your colleagues in their professional learning journeys?

KEY TAKEAWAYS

- Educator learning accelerates student learning.
- Barriers to professional learning can be interpersonal, intrapersonal, and structural.
- Perfectionism, criticism, blame, competition, fixed mindsets, burnout, lack of time and structure for collaboration, and initiative fatigue are some of the mindsets, behaviors, and dynamics that disrupt professional learning.
- Self-care and collective care support professional learning by reducing burnout.
- De-implementation is the reduction or elimination of practices that are ineffective, no longer useful, or cause harm. De-implementation can reduce initiative fatigue and create space for learning and innovation.
- Effective professional development is relevant to the needs of educators and equips them with concrete strategies and practices.
- Educators learn best when they learn from and with one another. Teacher-to-teacher collaboration, coaching, PLCs, constructive feedback, and peer mentoring facilitate educator learning.
- Learning is risky. We reduce that risk by asking questions, admitting what we don't know, maintaining a growth mindset, encouraging one another, researching and implementing evidence-based strategies, piloting new practices, learning from mistakes, and celebrating small wins.

PRACTICES, STRATEGIES, AND TOOLS

Individual Educator
• Practice learning behaviors, such as asking questions, admitting when you don't know something, researching and sharing evidence-based practices. • Be mindful of your mindset. Do you view challenging circumstances as fixed, or do you see possibilities for growth? • Avoid the seductive trap of blame. When things do not go as hoped, acknowledge your pain, frustration, or disappointment. Empower yourself by deciding on what you will do to address or improve the situation. Consider extending compassion to yourself and anyone else involved. • Be willing to grow. Try new strategies and collect evidence of impact. Celebrate small wins. • Notice your tone, body language, and the content of the feedback that you give to colleagues and how they receive it. Avoid criticism or personal attacks. Provide feedback that is specific, goal directed, encouraging, and consensual. • Invite, acknowledge, and integrate feedback from colleagues. Let colleagues know the specific topic(s) that you would like feedback on. If there are ways that they can deliver the feedback that are more easily digestible for you, let them know. Receive their feedback with self-compassion, self-respect, a growth mindset, and a willingness to do better. • When collaborating with colleagues, encourage them to share their ideas, questions, and concerns.
Team
• Encourage one another to share ideas, questions, and concerns. • Discuss problems of practice and brainstorm ways to address them. • Research and implement evidence-based practices. When implementing a strategy, collect and share evidence of impact. Celebrate small wins. • Share roses, buds, and thorns. • Resist blame and feeling defeated by disappointing student outcomes. Acknowledge your hard work. Treat this information as an opportunity to learn and grow. • Develop agreements for how you will give and receive constructive feedback within your team. • Engage in practices that facilitate professional learning for educators, such as learning walks, pineapple charts, microteaching, peer mentoring, and so on.

Administrator

- Research and implement practices and protocols that facilitate educator learning. Structured PLCs, learning walks, pineapple charts, microteaching, coaching, peer mentoring, classroom observations, all of which have been shown to increase educators' knowledge and skills.
- Reflect on school data and listen to educators to determine and provide relevant professional development.
- Check in on staff well-being throughout the year. Encourage and practice self-care. Work with your staff to identify and implement school-wide collective care practices.
- Pilot new practices to allow educators the opportunity to learn, make mistakes, and gradually develop mastery.
- De-implement school-wide practices and programs that are proven ineffective, no longer useful, or cause harm.
- Model learning behaviors for staff by asking questions, admitting when you don't know something, researching and sharing evidence-based practices.
- Constructive feedback matters. Seek out resources about providing quality feedback such as the book, *Better Feedback for Better Teaching*.[10]
- Ask for feedback on your leadership style using a variety of methods (e.g., anonymous staff surveys, one-on-one conversations, leadership coaching, etc.) to facilitate your own professional learning and growth.

6

CONTRIBUTOR SAFETY

Take a moment to read through the following scenarios and think about what they have in common.

- Every time Teresa suggests a new instructional strategy for her professional learning community to try, her suggestions are criticized or quickly dismissed with statements like, "That'll never work."
- Deborah is a paraprofessional who for the past 3 years has been assigned to work one-on-one with a student with severe disabilities. Every year, the student's Individualized Education Program (IEP) is updated, and no one on the IEP team asks Deborah for her input. When she takes the initiative to offer recommendations, her suggestions are ignored even though she works more closely with this student than anyone else at the school.
- Brightwood High School is high performing. Teachers are so busy working to sustain and improve student outcomes that they never have the opportunity to celebrate the results of their hard work.
- The administration at Devonshire Elementary surveys their staff to death. They send out surveys about every topic imaginable. However, after these surveys are completed, the staff never hears anything about the results, and there never seem to be any actions taken in response to their feedback.

- Gilberto's grade-level team meetings are dominated by two teachers who talk the entire time and never give anyone else an opportunity to share. These two teachers will vent, commiserate, and sometimes make decisions that affect the entire team without making space for anyone else to speak.
- Vishal has been teaching full time for 5 years and still doesn't make enough money to support his family. To supplement his income, he works a second job during the week and occasionally picks up shifts at a buddy's restaurant on the weekends.
- Joan, who we met in Chapter 1, works in a school where teachers feel overworked and unappreciated. They receive little acknowledgment from their administrator, and the staff have lost the sense of community they once had.

In these scenarios, the contributions that are made by these educators are either criticized, ignored, unacknowledged, trivialized, silenced, exploited, or undervalued. These scenarios describe a lack of contributor safety in the workplace. Contributor safety refers to welcoming and valuing each person's talents, skills, engagement, and impact in the workplace. By valuing, I mean both day-to-day acts of appreciation as well as financial compensation in terms of salary and benefits. Many educators work in schools and districts with devastatingly low levels of contributor safety. Over time, the lack of appreciation and the high demand of the work can leave them feeling exhausted, unappreciated, and disrespected. Their energy becomes invested in surviving their job rather than thriving in their vocation. For some, the spark of inspiration that brought them into this field is extinguished by the conditions they encounter while working in it, and they leave the profession.

A STAFFING AND COMPENSATION CRISIS

As I write this book, we are experiencing a national staffing shortage among education professionals in the United States. School districts across the country are struggling to fill vacancies for every position, from principal to classroom teacher to bus driver. Many districts are also experiencing a substitute teacher shortage, adding yet another challenge to the staffing crisis. Many educators have chosen to retire early or leave the profession. Unfortunately, fewer people are entering the field of education to fill these gaps.

In 2022, the American Association of Colleges for Teacher Education (AACTE) reported that the number of bachelor's degrees earned in education has decreased by 22% since 2005, whereas the number of undergraduate degrees awarded in other large career fields has risen by as much as 29%. As a result, some colleges and universities have elected to close their teacher preparation programs, whereas others are looking for new ways to attract students and remove barriers to enrollment. The AACTE found that low teacher pay and concerns about the conditions that educators face in schools are the top reasons why fewer people are choosing to enter the field.[1] The challenges that our education system is facing when it comes to recruiting and retaining teachers are evidence of a crisis of contributor safety. The financial and emotional costs of teaching are driving people away from the field.

Many career fields hope that professionals will go above and beyond what is asked of them in their job descriptions. Teaching requires that we do. I have never met an educator who could complete the requirements of their job within the workday. Educators work before the first bell, after the last bell, and take their work home over the weekend. Many teachers spend their own money on classroom materials and supplemental supplies for their students. In recent years, I have talked with educators around the country who are expected to plan lessons, differentiate instruction, manage behaviors, mediate conflict, analyze data, serve on multiple school committees, counsel struggling students, mentor new colleagues, regularly communicate with parents, connect families in need with community resources, de-escalate crises, provide mental health first aid, track the spread of a pandemic, and fight off active shooters. It is as though educators have become first responders, expected to catch every child who falls through the cracks created by a society that is failing its children.

When educators express their dissatisfaction and overwhelm at work, many are told that the solution to their discontent is self-care. As we discussed in Chapter 2, although self-care is essential, it is not enough. Self-care does not address the root causes of the problem unless you consider that the greatest act of self-care may be self-advocacy. In 2018, we saw an unprecedented number of educator walkouts and strikes across the United States. These acts of self- and collective advocacy demanded, and often won, improved working conditions and compensation for educators as well as more funding and resources for students.[2] On a systemic level, contributor safety cannot be achieved until every teacher is adequately paid and every school is equitably resourced.

Teachers help create every profession, yet for decades the rate increase of teachers' salaries has consistently and significantly fallen below the rate of inflation. Research conducted by the Economic Policy Institute (EPI) on teacher compensation has shown that from 1996 to 2021, the average weekly pay for teachers increased approximately $29 a week (adjusted for inflation); whereas the average inflation-adjusted weekly pay for other college graduates increased approximately $445 over the same time period. There is not a single state in which a public school teacher earns as much as the average nonteaching college graduate. In some states, teachers make as much as 35% less than other professionals who have similar levels of education.

It is worth noting that the employee benefits teachers receive do not offset this significant wage gap. Even after accounting for employee benefits, the EPI found that as of 2021 the average U.S. public school teacher received 14.2% less total compensation (salary with benefits) than other college-educated professionals. It is no wonder that so many educators work two and even three jobs to make ends meet, not to mention that many of them work in school districts that fail to provide quality insurance coverage, paid time off (e.g., parental leave, family medical leave, etc.), childcare assistance, social security enrollment, and retirement benefits. Some researchers have termed this compensation gap a "pay penalty."[3] In other words, individuals are financially punished with lower rates of compensation for choosing to work in the field of education. This pay penalty is one of the top reasons that college students give for choosing a career path other than education. It is a sad reality that people are punished for caring about children, who in John F. Kennedy's words, "are the world's most valuable resource and best hope for the future."[4]

The exploitation of educators is intimately connected with the underfunding of public schools, and both trends are rooted in public policy. In 1973, the U.S. Supreme Court decided in *San Antonio Independent School District v. Rodriguez* that education is not a fundamental right under the Constitution; therefore, schools are not entitled to equitable funding.[5] More recent Supreme Court decisions, such as *Carson v. Makin* and *Espinoza v. Montana Department of Revenue*, have further eroded funding for public education in favor of tax-credit and voucher programs that allow public taxpayer dollars to be spent on private schools.[6] As I write this, legislators and lobbyists in several states are pushing policies to divert taxpayer dollars from public schools into private institutions. Students and teachers, especially those in low-income communities, suffer the consequences of these policies.

When schools are systemically under-resourced, the professionals who work in schools can suffer moral trauma. As we discussed in Chapter 2, moral trauma is experienced when an educator knows that their students need a better quality of education and care, but they work in schools that don't have the resources to provide it. I think of a teacher who once said to me with tears in her eyes, "I work at my school from seven in the morning until seven at night. I am on multiple committees. I work on the weekends. It is still not enough. My students need more than I can give, and that breaks my heart." This educator, like countless educators across the country, was experiencing the pain of working in a system where, despite our best intentions, we don't have the resources to provide our students with the education and care they need and deserve.

To address the inequities we see in our classrooms, we must hold our elected officials accountable. Our elected officials work for us, yet they have failed to do their job when it comes to supporting our nation's education system. Vote for candidates who have a commitment and a plan to fully fund public education. Also, if you have the option, consider joining your local union or teachers' association because they often do the important work of advocating for the needs of educators. I apologize if this feels like a bit of a political rant, but we will never recruit, retain, *and* value quality educators until we appropriately compensate them for their work. Having said that, contributor safety for educators extends beyond financial compensation to include workplace practices that encourage and value the contributions of each professional. In the rest of this chapter, we will explore ways that each of us can help build a culture of contributor safety within our schools through teamwork, accountability, and appreciation.

REFLECTION QUESTIONS

1. Can you relate to any of the scenarios listed at the beginning of this chapter? What are some of the ways that contributor safety, or a lack of it, show up in your school?
2. When you feel overwhelmed by the responsibilities and demands associated with being an educator, how do you care for yourself? How do you advocate for your needs and the needs of your students?

IT TAKES A VILLAGE

When it comes to creating quality schools, it truly takes a village. No single educator can run a school alone; we need the talents and gifts that each of our colleagues brings to the learning community. As I mentioned in previous chapters, high-performing schools have high levels of collective teacher efficacy, meaning that educators in these schools collaborate effectively to improve student outcomes. The power of collective efficacy points to the fact that high-performing schools honor the interdependent nature of their work. Interdependence in the workplace occurs when professionals work independently but also rely on one another to achieve success. When we depend on one another, we are accountable to each other. When someone doesn't follow through on their part of the work, it affects the rest of the team. This balance between autonomy and accountability is at the heart of effective teamwork.

In his theory of psychological safety in the workplace, Thomas R. Clark has proposed that contributor safety is earned. For Clark, contributor safety is a trade-off: as an employee proves their effectiveness through the results they produce, they receive more autonomy.[7] However, I have found that for schools, the relationship between autonomy and results functions differently. I have worked with schools where highly effective teachers earn greater autonomy as their students show proficiency and growth. This decision to grant autonomy in exchange for evidence of impact makes sense in education but only to a point. When it comes to contributor safety in schools, there needs to be a balance between autonomy and interdependence.

Here is an example. I once worked with a large urban high school that had the highest-performing science teacher in the city. His students outperformed the students of every other science teacher in the district and significantly surpassed the average passing rates on state assessments. When I visited other classrooms in his school, the teachers had certain common practices that they adhered to: Class periods started with a "do now" assignment, students sat and worked in groups, and every class period ended with some form of an exit ticket or check for understanding. The school administration would observe their classrooms and evaluate their adherence to and implementation of these practices. His classroom, however, was its own world. Each class period started with a quiz. Students sat in rows and worked independently until the bell rang. Because of his success record, he was allowed to run his classroom however he chose. It was interesting to then observe the dynamics of the science department meetings because the rest of the teachers would common plan and he would keep to himself. Often, he'd be grading papers while everyone else was discussing an instructional topic or reviewing assessment data.

On the one hand, I think of the expression, "If it isn't broken, don't fix it." This science teacher was teaching in a way that fit his style, and his students were successful, so changing that in the interest of increasing conformity among the science teachers would not have made much sense. There is merit to granting more autonomy based upon evidence of success while providing teachers who are struggling more scaffolded support and accountability to foster student achievement. However, this dynamic should not go to such an extreme that teachers lose common ground. In the case of this science teacher, he became so disconnected from the rest of his department that it eroded collaboration. He and his colleagues could have benefitted from sharing strategies and developing common practices to foster achievement for all their students. For that to happen, there would have to be a willingness, among both teachers and administrators, to find a middle ground between shared practices and individual differences in teaching styles. In other words, if data shows that a practice is effective in supporting student learning, then keep doing it (and share it with colleagues), and if it isn't effective, then work *together* to find an approach that is.

I've seen schools where autonomy is freely and excessively granted without proof of success. Each teacher runs their classroom however they choose. The result is a school in which students achieve success by chance rather than by design. Parents must play the lottery each year, hoping their child gets one of the "good teachers," because if they don't, then they will likely struggle. Success by design is built on interdependence. Teachers have a certain degree of autonomy while also working together to implement best practices throughout their school.

On the other extreme, I have worked with schools where teachers have little to no autonomy. The school culture is driven by an obsession with compliance and tedium. Educators are micromanaged to the degree that it stifles their passion, talent, and creativity. This extreme is equally harmful to students because part of a quality education is each student receiving what they need to be successful, which necessitates differentiation and innovation. Education is not a one-size-fits-all approach. Demanding absolute conformity among a teaching staff is not a sign of interdependence; it's a misuse of power.

In schools with a healthy sense of interdependence, teachers have their own styles while also working together to implement common curriculum, expectations, and practices that are in the best interests of their students. Here is another example. I worked with a large urban middle school that had a robust and successful behavior system. The school had clear expectations and common practices for promoting positive behavior and redirecting challenging behaviors. Every part of this system was clearly defined for teachers, including the types of additional support they could receive if a student's behaviors persisted despite their efforts in the classroom. When new staff were hired, they received considerable training on the school's behavior system. All staff were observed by the administration throughout the school year. They received feedback and support in implementing the school-wide behavioral supports and practices.

Now here is where things get real. The behavior system was a lot of work. The school used a points system to reinforce its positive behavioral expectations. Every student started each school day with 100 points. They lost points each time their behavior had to be redirected by someone on the school staff. Students could use their points to earn individual incentives (e.g., like dress down passes because this school had uniforms), or they could pool their points with classmates to earn whole class incentives (e.g., a movie day). The behavior system also had a four-level redirection protocol that teachers had to follow when responding to challenging behaviors. Level 1 was a verbal warning; Level 2 was a one-on-one conversation; Level 3 was an opportunity for a student to take a brief break, reflect, and start again; Level 4 was a restorative conversation with the dean and a parent contact. Every teacher in the school was required to implement both the reinforcement (points) and the redirection practices in their classroom.

I must admit, as someone who isn't a big fan of school-wide systems of extrinsic rewards and incentives, the school's behavior system worked. It worked because the adults in the building were on the same page and they each did their part to implement the practices consistently. Time and again I have found the student behavior improves the degree to which adults are consistent in how they respond to it. This staff was consistent, and they had the evidence to prove that their efforts made a difference. Prior to introducing their system, the school struggled with severe behavioral issues. It had a high number of suspensions each year and a reputation in the community for being a school that was run by student misbehavior. Since implementing the system, suspensions dropped by nearly 80%, overall academic performance improved considerably, and parents now celebrate the fact that their kids get to attend this middle school.

However, when I asked the staff how they felt about the behavior system, their responses were surprisingly lukewarm. They said it was a lot of work. Several of them said they found it difficult to be consistent and to not give into their own moods and frustrations. As one teacher said, "Sometimes I get annoyed with a kid, and I want to skip from Level 1 to Level 4, but I can't." Some teachers said that adjusting to the system was challenging because it didn't fit their personality or their teaching style. So, I asked them, "Why do you still do it if it's so difficult?" One teacher summed up the feelings of the group when she said, "We're not classroom teachers. We are school teachers." She went on, "It's our job to uphold our school's expectations in our classrooms, in the hallways, throughout our campus." She explained that when everyone did their part to implement the behavior system, it made their jobs easier. The staff wasn't breaking up fights all day or wasting instructional time constantly redirecting behaviors. Teachers knew how to respond to students' behavioral issues; they didn't experience anxiety from having to figure out how to respond to a student's behavior. There was also a clear sense that the staff had each other's back because they were all engaged in the same work. As a result, students knew what was expected of them, and the consistency created an environment that was optimal for teaching and learning.

REFLECTION QUESTIONS

1. Do you think instructional autonomy should be granted to teachers based on student achievement? Why or why not?
2. What is the relationship between autonomy and interdependence within your school? To what extent do educators do their own thing versus implement common practices and expectations?

SUCCESS BY DESIGN, NOT BY CHANCE

Listening to her, I understood that their behavior system was success by design. Every teacher was on the same page. If a teacher decided to forgo the behavior system and do their own thing, they'd be setting their students up to struggle and abandoning their colleagues. By choosing to uphold the behavior system, each member of staff contributed something valuable to the entire school community. Each of the educators did their part and relied on their colleagues to do the same. This level of interdependence was sustained by a high degree of accountability among the staff.

Some educators hold negative perceptions of accountability, associating it with punishment, micromanagement, and faultfinding. These misperceptions are typically formed because of experiences they have had working with fear-based administrators in schools with low levels of psychological safety. Accountability in psychologically safe schools can feel uncomfortable at times, especially when someone has failed to fulfill their professional duties; however, it should never be wielded in ways that are demeaning, unfair, or abusive. In psychologically safe schools, accountability is rooted in relationships, shared goals, mutual support, and clearly defined roles and responsibilities.

Thomas R. Clark defines three levels of accountability within the workplace that are central to contributor safety. These levels are task, process, and outcome.[8] When I apply this to schools, I think of it this way: the what, the how, and the result of our work. Task accountability for educators involves completing the tasks that help the school operate from day to day. These tasks include the basics, which may look like following the daily schedule, managing arrival and dismissal, monitoring the hallways during transitions, and other duties that keep a school running. Process accountability refers to how we do our work. Process accountability encompasses the ways we implement pedagogical, behavioral, and social-emotional practices in our classrooms and throughout our schools. Last, outcome accountability is the responsibility we share for student outcomes such as discipline data, graduation rates, attendance, and academic outcomes.

Schools can have various degrees of task, process, and outcome accountability. For example, staff could devote considerable effort to raising standardized test scores (outcome accountability) but neglect to monitor and manage the hallways, cafeteria, and common areas (task responsibility), which then become chaotic. In the next chapter, we'll explore what happens when there is a lack of accountability in schools and the frustration, resentment, and conflict that can ensue among colleagues. For now, I want us to focus on the positive impact of accountability. Educators cultivate and sustain accountability when they fulfill their roles and responsibilities and when they keep the promises and commitments that they make to one another.

Accountability among a staff fosters trust and motivation. When there is a high level of accountability, educators know they can depend upon on one another, and they are more willing to invest their time, energy, and effort. Accountability invites contribution.

There are times when we encounter challenges in our schools the require us to go beyond our prescribed roles and responsibilities and to innovate and develop new strategies or practices. Perhaps a crisis or scarcity of resources leads us to find another way to go about meeting a need. Educators accomplished a great deal of innovation when they transitioned from in-person to virtual instruction at the onset of the COVID-19 pandemic. However, there may be other times when we innovate because we are inspired by the possibility of providing our students with a better education or access to opportunity. For example, many districts have developed new programs that increase students' access to technology and provide opportunities to build new skills like coding, video game design, and so on. Regardless of whether the innovation is proactive or reactive, the process of innovation is more likely to be successful when educators are invited and encouraged to contribute their ideas, talents, and insights.

Welcoming one another's input is an act of contributor safety that we can practice anytime we meet with our colleagues to work together as a team. In the beginning of this chapter, we reviewed a series of brief scenarios in which the contributions of educators were devalued, criticized, or ignored. One way to make sure that your team meetings are psychologically safe spaces for educators is to engage in practices that invite and respect each member's participation. I've compiled a list of practices that you and your colleagues can put into action when you meet as a team.

Contributor Safety Team Tool Kit

- **Establish Communication Agreements:** Establish communication agreements that ensure respectful dialogue and equity of voice. As a team, come up with a plan for what to do if or when they aren't being upheld. Read them at the start of every team meeting, and revisit them as needed. One of those agreements can be that team members share airtime to allow for others to speak. Another agreement could be to use a talking piece when conversations become energized and team members find themselves talking over one another.
- **Use Technology Appropriately:** As a team, decide on what types of technology use are appropriate during meetings.

(Continued)

(Continued)

- **Ask Versus Tell:** Notice how much you ask questions versus tell others what you think. Try to find a balance. For some of us this means being more assertive about our ideas, whereas for others it may mean stepping back, asking questions, and listening more.
- **Speak Last:** This strategy is for anyone who holds a leadership position within the school or on the team. If you share your opinion early in the conversation, then people with differing perspectives may choose to be silent out of respect for the power you have in the group. Allow other members of the team to share before you chime into the conversation.
- **Honor Think Time:** When talking about complex or important topics, give yourself and your colleagues a few moments to pause and reflect. You can put this into your team's meeting agenda or even say out loud, "Before we discuss this any further, let's take a moment to gather our thoughts."
- **Encourage Spectators to Play:** Ask the team if anyone else would like to speak before moving on or making a final decision. Over time you may notice that some team members hardly ever speak up. This doesn't mean that they aren't engaged. Talk with your colleagues, ask for their input, and encourage them to share their ideas.
- **Listen for the Gold:** To avoid criticizing or dismissing what someone has shared, try to find something of value in what they shared and acknowledge it. Even if you don't agree with their perspective, the gold may be that they are passionate about the topic.
- **Follow-Up to Follow-Through:** This strategy is especially important for school leadership teams. If you gather input from colleagues, whether it is through an email, focus group, discussion, or survey, follow up in a timely manner by sharing what you learned from their responses. This will help ensure that you accurately understood their input and didn't miss or misinterpret anything important. If their feedback reveals that your team needs to take action, then make an action plan and share that plan with those involved. Sharing the action plan with others will increase accountability and follow-through.

I invite you and your colleagues to add to this list of practices as you discover new ways to enhance the quality of your communication. To create psychologically safe teams, it is important that we not only invite each member to contribute but that we value those contributions as well.

You may recall in Chapter 1, we met Joan, a hardworking educator who felt deeply hurt by the lack of acknowledgment and appreciation she received at work. In the months following that tearful phone call, Joan and I checked in periodically. During one of our conversations, she told me that the morale in her school was low in general. Teachers were exhausted, and the school had lost the sense of community it once had. She said, "Teachers show up to do their job, and they leave. We used to have baby showers and birthday celebrations for one another. If somebody needed something, we helped each other out. Now, you rarely hear someone say, 'Thank you.' If someone jams the copier, they leave it for the next person to deal with it. The whole feeling of togetherness is gone." The feeling of community and interdependence in Joan's school had diminished because the staff was overworked and underappreciated.

REFLECTION QUESTIONS

1. How is professional accountability handled within your school?
2. Look over the Contributor Safety Team Tool Kit. Which one of the practices would be the most helpful to the team(s) that you are on? Why?

GRATITUDE AND APPRECIATION

In the words of CEO and executive coach Naz Beheshti, "Gratitude is a recognition of our interdependence, of the fact that success is the result of team effort."[9] None of us can run a school by ourselves. We need one another in our work as educators. When we express gratitude at work, it elevates even the most basic tasks from acts of compliance or obligation to stewardship of our school community.

Gratitude benefits the giver as much as the receiver. Expressing gratitude has been shown to have a positive impact on mood, physical health, sleep, and even metabolism. People who regularly express gratitude tend to be happier and have fewer stress-related illnesses.[10] Studies have shown that when people feel appreciated in their workplace, they are more likely to go the extra mile. Their levels of motivation, productivity, and engagement at work increase as a result of feeling valued.[11] Gratitude has also been shown to reduce symptoms of burnout among teachers.[12] One study even found that as expressions of gratitude increased among colleagues, workplace mistreatment and bullying behaviors decreased.[13] Thankfully gratitude in the workplace can be contagious. When someone feels appreciated at work, they are more likely to pay it forward by expressing gratitude toward their colleagues. Although Teacher Appreciation Week and other weeks that honor the contributions of school employees are important, gratitude becomes a transformative practice when it is expressed throughout the school year.

Transforming School Culture Through Gratitude

Here are a few suggestions for cultivating contributor safety and improving school culture through gratitude. These suggestions are especially helpful for school administrators but can be useful to all staff members.

1. **Celebrate the Person, Not Only the Product**: Celebrating successes boosts morale. However, gratitude should also be expressed to individuals for the unique skills, talents, effort, and heart they bring to their work, not only the results they produce.
2. **Be Sincere**: Generic, rote expressions of gratitude in the workplace can feel patronizing and even manipulative. Expressions of gratitude, even simple ones (e.g., a few words of thanks) are most impactful when they are sincere and specific.
3. **Tolerate Discomfort**: For some people, expressing or receiving gratitude can feel awkward and uncomfortable. When we express gratitude, we are admitting that other peoples' words and actions affect us, albeit in a positive way, but it is still an acknowledgment of our vulnerability. Receiving gratitude is like being offered a gift, and accepting it graciously is an act of kindness, respect, and mutuality. Fortunately, the benefits of expressing and receiving gratitude are worth the cost of any momentary discomfort.
4. **Honor Multiple Gratitude Languages**: Gratitude has been compared to love languages, meaning that people have different ways of expressing and receiving it. Explore different ways to express gratitude to colleagues, such as acts of kindness, words of affirmation, thoughtful gifts, and so on.
5. **Small and Frequent Beats Big and Rare**: When it comes to building a culture of gratitude in your school, small and frequent expressions of appreciation have a greater impact on school culture than events that happen once or twice a year. Not that your school must choose between big or small acts of appreciation—in fact, it is best to have a mix of both. For example, you and your colleagues can celebrate staff appreciation events while also finding simple ways to express gratitude in staff meetings, communications (e.g., emails, newsletters, etc.), and one-on-one interactions throughout the school year.

To experience the benefits of gratitude, you can begin with yourself and then share gratitude with others. In the previous chapter, I mentioned Dr. Bryan Sexton, a researcher who studies workplace well-being. Dr. Sexton's research has revealed the power of bite-size resilience strategies, simple practices that only take a few minutes but have a big impact on our well-being. He and his colleagues have found that these practices can prevent and alleviate burnout. One of the most powerful bite-size resilience practices is Three Good Things. For 2 weeks, ideally just before bed, write down three good things that occurred that day and reflect on why they happened. As you practice Three Good Things, you may notice your thinking shift more toward the positive as your brain increasingly looks for good things throughout each day. Researchers have found that Three Good Things alleviates stress, emotional exhaustion, and burnout for several months after completing the two weeks.[14]

Another bite-size resilience strategy is writing a gratitude letter. This doesn't have to be a formal letter; it can be a card, note, email, or text message. Simply sit for a few minutes and think of someone you are thankful for. Reflect on what it is that you appreciate about them; this may be something that they did or said or a quality that they possess. Then spend a few minutes writing them a brief message of thanks. Research shows that taking the time to reflect and write a gratitude message is enough to have a positive impact on your well-being.[15] By sharing your message of gratitude, you are letting that person know that they are seen and valued. I encourage you to try this strategy and let a colleague know that you appreciate them. Go for it, and risk starting an outbreak of gratitude in your workplace. Saying thank-you, acts of kindness, notes of appreciation, all these little acts of gratitude can create a school community where everyone feels valued.

I'd like to close the chapter by coming back to Joan. In one of our conversations, she said that the passion she once had for teaching has disappeared. Since that call, she decided to search for her spark and found it in a side business that she started as an event planner. She enjoys this new type of work. It gives her a sense of vitality that teaching no longer provides, likely because she feels valued and appreciated by her clients. In our most recent conversation, she was hopeful that the income from this new business venture will be enough for her to leave the teaching profession. My fear is that other schools will lose valuable educators like Joan because they fail to value them.

REFLECTION QUESTIONS

1. Who is someone at your school whom you are thankful for? Why do you feel this gratitude for them? Is there some way you can let them know?
2. What are three good things that happened today, and how did they come about?

KEY TAKEAWAYS

- Contributor safety refers to welcoming and valuing each person's talents, skills, engagement, and impact in the workplace.
- On a systemic level, contributor safety cannot be achieved until every teacher is adequately paid and every school is equitably resourced.
- Psychologically safe schools balance interdependence and autonomy.
- In psychologically safe schools, accountability is rooted in relationships, shared goals, mutual support, and clearly defined roles and responsibilities.
- When educators know that they can depend upon one another, they are more willing to invest their time, energy, and effort.
- Contributor safety facilitates educational innovation.
- School teams cultivate contributor safety by communicating in ways that encourage each team member to share and participate.
- Bite-size resilience practices alleviate symptoms of burnout and support well-being.
- Gratitude fosters resilience and transforms workplace culture.

PRACTICES, STRATEGIES, AND TOOLS

Individual Educator
• Cultivate a sense of pride and ownership in your work. Notice the difference that you make. Keep the thank-you notes and mementos that fill your heart. Being an educator is an extraordinary profession. • In a journal or the notes app of your phone, jot down meaningful experiences you have as an educator. Read them when you need a dose of inspiration. • Add to them as much as possible. • Express appreciation and gratitude to your colleagues. • Compliment colleagues for their skills, talents, and insights. • Avoid body language and statements that demean other people, such as sarcasm, eye-rolling, looking at your phone during meetings and conversations, "I told you so," and so on. • Practice the communication strategies in the Contributor Safety Team Tool Kit. • Advocate for your professional needs. Remember that one of the most powerful approaches to advocacy is to negotiate win-win outcomes rather than burning bridges. • Practice bite-size resilience through small acts of kindness, gratitude notes, and Three Good Things.
Team
• Practice the communication strategies in the Contributor Safety Team Tool Kit. • Find opportunities to express gratitude and celebrate your impact as a team. • Encourage one another to share strategies and new ideas. • Acknowledge when the team is stuck. If the team doesn't know how to respond to a challenging topic, move the conversation toward determining how the team could arrive at greater clarity. Sometimes conversations need to be paused and returned to when more information is available or emotions have settled. • Celebrate student growth as well as proficiency. What appears to be a small learning gain may be a huge achievement for some students—and worth celebrating. • Share good things. At the end of a meeting, ask each team member to share one good thing that happened recently at school. You may wish to pass around a piece of paper or sticky notes, so each person can write down their good thing and the team can post them.

Administrator
• Foster accountability by building positive relationships, articulating shared goals, clearly communicating expectations, giving constructive feedback, and providing support. • Practice the communication strategies in the Contributor Safety Team Tool Kit. • Celebrate student growth as well as proficiency. • Express gratitude to staff, and acknowledge their skills, talents, insights, and hard work. Specific and genuine expressions of appreciation are the most meaningful. • Practice Three Good Things. Share at least three good things about a staff member when giving them feedback. Celebrate three (or more) good things as a staff at the end of each month. Share the Three Good Things strategy in a newsletter. • Start off staff meetings by having staff pair up and share one example of student progress that inspires them and what they did to help make it happen. Remind them that all forms of progress (e.g., academic, relational, behavioral, etc.), great and small, are worth celebrating. • Thoughtfully acknowledge significant events in the lives of staff members (e.g., marriages, family illnesses, etc.). • Be mindful of your body language, tone, and content of your communication. Avoid communicating in ways that demean, threaten, or disregard staff members. • Lead in a way that honors autonomy and interdependence. Allow teachers to express their own talents and teaching styles while also holding them accountable to the school's shared expectations and practices.

7

CHALLENGER SAFETY

In the words of Timothy R. Clark, "Challenger Safety is a level of psychological safety so high that people feel empowered to challenge the status quo, leaving their comfort zones to put a creative or disruptive idea on the table, which by definition, is a threat to the way things are done and therefore a risk to themselves personally."[1] Challenger safety is the pinnacle of psychological safety. Challenging the status quo may involve disrupting practices that are ineffective or harmful to students and developing new ways of doing things. When we engage in disruption and innovation, we make ourselves vulnerable to criticism and failure: What if our ideas don't work? What if we experience backlash because someone is angered by our efforts to create change? Challenger safety enables individuals and teams to take the risk of implementing new practices with the assurance that even if those practices don't produce the outcomes we hoped for, the experience will still be treated as an opportunity to learn and grow.

At times, challenging the status quo may be less about innovation and change and more about accountability and following through on the actions that we have individually or collectively agreed upon. Some educators work in schools or on teams that "punish the good." In these environments, hard-working educators find themselves picking up the slack for their less productive colleagues. More work is assigned to individuals who follow through on their professional commitments, whereas their colleagues get away with cutting corners and/or noncompliance. Over time, this inequitable distribution of work causes teams to fragment as resentments fester among colleagues and the hardest-working individuals become the most susceptible to burnout. These work environments lack a sense of shared responsibility and accountability among staff, which makes it nearly impossible to effectively address problems and challenges that arise within the school. Later in this chapter, we will explore the role accountability plays in developing and sustaining challenger safety.

Working in a school that has challenger safety can be uncomfortable at times. In these schools, educators routinely challenge themselves and one another to continually improve their ability to meet the needs of their students. Challenger safety in schools encompasses the ways that educators challenge the status quo, address challenges through respectful and productive collaboration, maintain and restore individual and collective accountability, and navigate interpersonal conflict. Challenger safety facilitates professional growth and evolution, which is never easy. However, working in a school that doesn't have challenger safety can be spirit crushing.

Let's imagine that you start a new position teaching in a school where students are performing far below grade level and exhibiting out-of-control behaviors, rates of chronic absenteeism are high, and parent engagement is nearly nonexistent. In fact, the only thing lower than the rate of parent engagement is staff morale. Most of your colleagues feel resigned, cynical, and defeated. Unfortunately, every time you make the slightest suggestion for how things might be done differently, your ideas are ridiculed and dismissed by your colleagues. This dynamic continues from year to year as the hope you once felt hardens into cynicism and resignation, your passion for teaching eventually surrenders to disappointment and despair, and your growth mindset gets beaten down. These are the costs of working in a school that lacks challenger safety.

REFLECTION QUESTIONS

1. Is there a school-wide policy or practice that you feel is harmful or ineffective? What do you think could be done to disrupt and transform it?
2. Do you feel that your school has an equitable distribution of work and shared sense of responsibility among staff? Why or why not?

NICE ISN'T ALWAYS KIND

In Chapter 1 we discussed Toni, the principal of a large K-8 school, and the dynamics of her school's fifth grade team. As you may recall, the workplace culture of Toni's school prized "niceness" above all else. I want to be clear that by "niceness" I do not mean kindness. In fact, "nice" schools are often unkind places to work and are rife with backhanded compliments, gossip, and backstabbing. By "niceness," I mean the avoidance of authentic communication, vulnerability, and productive conflict through superficial interactions that maintain the status quo. For example, when Toni's fifth grade team met in their weekly professional learning community (PLC), the team avoided discussing how they could improve their instruction to support students who were not making progress. Toni made a point to observe each grade level's PLC once each month. During a meeting with her fifth grade team, she felt the need to intervene because an important conversation wasn't happening. Toni asked the team about the students who were not making progress, and she noticed that the tone of the meeting quickly shifted. Members of the team were suddenly quiet and seemed reluctant to share. A few teachers made comments about individual students whose behavior was disruptive and defiant, and another teacher spoke about a lack of involvement from her students' parents, especially the parents of her chronically absent students.

Toni noticed that the teachers didn't analyze the assessment data to uncover the gaps in their students' knowledge and skills. Instead, the team chose to focus on factors related to the behavior of the students and their parents. Toni asked the team if they were implementing the new district-adopted curricular materials with fidelity. The team assured her that they were. One of the teachers went as far as to add that adjusting to the new curriculum demanded considerable effort, but the team had worked diligently to support one another in making the transition. Toni wanted to ask how they were going to differentiate their instruction to support the students who were not making progress, but she could tell the topic made members of the team anxious, and she feared pushing them beyond their comfort zone. Toni backed away from the topic, and the team quickly pivoted to discuss an upcoming field trip.

Toni later learned through one-on-one conversations with the fifth grade teachers that the core curriculum was not being implemented with fidelity and the team members spent most of the time in their PLCs working in isolation as though it were their prep. One of the teachers shared privately with Toni that she was uncomfortable with the fact that members of her grade-level team were not implementing the new curriculum. One of her colleagues told her that he puts on a "dog and pony show" during observations to make it appear that he is faithfully utilizing the new curricular materials, then after the observation he goes back to teaching in the way that works best for him (not his students). Another teacher on the team told Toni that she was frustrated with the PLCs because they felt like a waste of time. Everyone was on their laptops writing emails, preparing lessons, but they never collaborated as a team. It felt pointless to her that they were forced to sit in the same room for an hour every week.

Toni reassured each of the teachers she spoke with that she would address their concerns, but honestly, she wasn't sure how she was going to do that. Toni managed her building by trying to make everyone happy. She figured that if her teachers liked her and they were happy to come to work, then they would be more likely to comply with her requests, and in theory this made sense. In practice, Toni found herself frequently making promises she knew she couldn't keep, saying things to appease one group of teachers that contradicted things she had said to other staff; even though she was technically the school leader, she felt like she was in service to the whims and moods of her staff. Worse still, her people-pleasing approach to leadership (a common fear-based "fawn" response) had failed to produce the results she hoped for. Instead of a happy, compliant staff, Toni knew that many of her teachers didn't respect her let alone comply with her requests and initiatives. Teachers were almost always pleasant and agreeable to her face, but she suspected that they criticized her mercilessly behind her back, and she knew that many of them covertly disregarded or resisted her directives. On some level, Toni empathized with even her harshest critics because she felt that at times her leadership lacked integrity, consistency, and follow-through. She tried to make up for this by doing nice things for her staff like buying them bagels and making a point to celebrate staff birthdays. When it came to ensuring compliance with school-wide initiatives, Toni generally avoided accountability conversations, partly out of a heartfelt, though overdeveloped, sense of responsibility for the well-being of her staff. She knew that her staff were overwhelmed by the already endless demands of teaching, and she hated adding one more thing to their plates. So, she avoided giving clear directives and having accountability conversations because she feared negative reactions from her staff.

Toni wasn't the only one in her school who avoided conflict. A superficial niceness permeated her school's workplace culture. There were many unappointed leaders in the building, teachers who didn't hold any formal positions as leaders within the school but had significant influence and social capital. They used that social capital to advocate for their personal agendas and squelch the expression of any disagreement, dissent, or point of view that was different from their own. This sort of unofficial pecking order allocated the greatest power and influence to staff who had been at the school the longest, making it especially difficult for newer teachers to feel welcomed and valued. It also made it nearly impossible for teachers to collaborate effectively and innovate when needed. The teachers at the top of this pecking order preferred to do things the way they had always done them and were quick to shut down any suggestions about ways to do things differently. They did this by playing nice during meetings only to later engage in merciless gossip, excessive criticism, social exclusion, and other forms of indirect and relational aggression. As I said, "nice" schools are rarely kind schools. Some degree of disagreement, frustration, and conflict is inevitable in the workplace; however, when conflict is avoided, or handled poorly, unresolved frustrations can fester into deep-seated resentments that fuel breakdowns in communication, ineffective teams, and workplace bullying behaviors.

The impact of this dynamic, as we saw among Toni's fifth grade team, was that meaningful conversations about gaps in student achievement and the need for instructional differentiation or innovation were avoided. In turn, ineffective instructional practices were continually implemented simply because they were familiar to the teachers at the top of the school's unspoken social hierarchy. Conversations during PLCs were relegated to "safe topics" such as venting about students, parents, or the administration or discussing field trips, school sports, or community events. If the topic of instruction was broached, it was not in the form of a collaborative inquiry into evidence-based best practices to address students' learning needs. Instead, teachers typically insisted that they were doing everything they could and that their students were struggling academically because of their behavior, their parents, their attendance, or the teacher(s) they had the previous school year. If the conversation got beyond admiring the problem, the only solution proposed by teachers was to refer chronically low-performing students for evaluation for special education or, if the student already had an IEP, then advocate for the student to be assigned a one-on-one paraprofessional.

REFLECTION QUESTIONS

1. How do you and your colleagues navigate tough conversations and challenges? Are there any work-related topics that are off limits or avoided?
2. What advice would you give to Toni on how to support her staff while also holding them accountable?

An effective PLC comprises a team of educators who engage in a structured inquiry process that is informed by evidence of impact, which drives pedagogical design and innovation, and results in measurable student progress. In an effective PLC, educators embrace the productive struggle that is inherent in collective efficacy. This productive struggle demands the willingness and ability to do the following:

- Unflinchingly analyze data while avoiding the seductive yet disempowering trap of blame
- Collectively identify growth areas and gaps in student outcomes without personal egos or agendas getting in the way
- Establish ambitious and attainable goals for student achievement
- Research evidence-based strategies and tools that may require educators to move beyond the familiar
- Consistently implement these evidence-based pedagogical practices despite competing demands and fatigue
- Refine your goals and practices according to evidence of impact, and celebrate progress

This process is possible only when there is a sufficient degree of challenger safety that enables teams to discuss difficult and complex topics, share multiple and at times differing perspectives, and productively navigate challenges in ways that facilitate effective action. This is hard work, and educators who work on productive teams accomplish it daily.

Famed musician Pat Benatar said "love is a battlefield"; well, so is teaching. Teaching can be painful, messy, baffling, and overwhelming. When educators work in schools with low levels of challenger safety, their energy is diverted from the productive struggle of collective efficacy into maintaining façades, managing interpersonal conflicts, and defending the status quo. Superficial niceness, pecking orders, and conflict avoidance are not the only barriers to challenger safety.

Some educators work in schools where challenging topics are discussed frequently and conflict is tackled head-on but not in ways that are respectful or productive. For example, a former colleague of mine worked in a wealthy private high school that he described as having a cover your ass (CYA) culture. He said that every educator at the school felt pressured to maintain the façade of being the "perfect teacher" who had all the answers and could manage everything on their own. That pressure was applied through faultfinding and punitive interactions among administrators and staff.

He told me that when a teacher expressed any frustrations to the administration about school-wide policies or practices, the administration would often retaliate by more frequently observing that teacher's classroom, looking for any opportunity to put the teacher on an improvement plan, or even terminating them. Worse still were the occasions when a parent complained to the administration about a teacher. He said that without fail the administration would take sides with the parent, not bothering to inquire about the teacher's perspective on the situation and move forward with a disciplinary action against the teacher, typically a letter in their file.

To maintain some sense of security within this faultfinding and antagonistic workplace culture (driven by a fear-based "fight" approach to leadership), my colleague said that he made every effort to protect himself from potential scrutiny or harm. He obsessively saved his lesson plans, maintained scrupulously detailed records of student data, saved copies of all his evaluations from administrators, kept notes in his phone concerning any disciplinary actions with students, saved work-related text messages and e-mails, and documented every communication with a parent or administrator.

He said that even among teachers, minor disagreements during department or grade-level team meetings would quickly turn personal, often escalating into long-standing feuds between staff members. He said to me, "I can't think of single meeting where someone didn't say something that was either an outright criticism of a colleague, a backhanded compliment, or an insult that was veiled as a question or advice. It felt like everyone was constantly trying to make themselves look a little bit better than everyone else." Whether it is feeling the relentless pressure to CYA or plastering a smile on your face and pretending things are fine when they aren't, these behaviors have one thing in common, fear. *Fear is the greatest barrier to psychological safety*: fear of criticism; fear of failure; fear of accountability; fear of losing power, influence, or respect; fear of punishment or retaliation; fear of change; fear of vulnerability.

When schools find themselves faced with significant challenges, whether it is persistent learning gaps, a lack of accountability and support when addressing student behaviors, or deep-seated divisions among the staff, they desperately need challenger safety. Educators must feel encouraged and safe enough to share ideas, challenge ineffective practices, innovate, and experiment. This is impossible to achieve in a fear-based culture that punishes people for speaking up or advocating for change. As a result, even when districts attempt to implement evidence-based initiatives to respond to the needs of students, many of those initiatives fail when educators withhold their energy and ideas. They do this not because they don't care about students but because they have chosen to protect themselves from burnout, conflict, and the cost of having to implement one more thing. So, they passively resist change; in turn the initiative fails, and yet another initiative is piled on. Now, the one more thing they were resisting has become two or three more things. Somewhere buried under the burden of all these initiatives and programs are educators who have not been given the time, opportunity, or structures to develop their collective expertise and impact. This requires schools to implement practices that reduce fear and create the conditions for collaboration, inquiry, experimentation, productive struggle, and innovation. Let's explore practices that facilitate the productive struggle necessary for collective growth and impact.

REFLECTION QUESTIONS

1. Fear is a natural human emotion. Being aware of our fears in a nonjudgmental fashion can help us know how to respond them. Are there any fears that show up for you when you collaborate with your colleagues? Do you think any of your colleagues have similar fears? What might help you and them to feel safe?
2. Have you ever worked in a school with a CYA staff culture? If so, what impact did it have on trust and collaboration among colleagues?

PSYCHOLOGICALLY SAFE PROTOCOLS

One of the most important steps that a team can take to foster challenger safety is to implement and maintain protocols for collaboration. Protocols provide a clear structure for the time educators spend collaborating with their colleagues. Protocols ensure that educators understand the purpose and structure of the collaborative process, which creates a sense of safety because educators know what is expected of them and how to prepare and engage accordingly. Protocols also ensure that educators know that their time is respected and valued. Unstructured meetings can quickly devolve into venting sessions and become a waste of time. As we saw in Toni's school, teachers met in PLCs because their schedule required it; however, the lack of structure compromised their effectiveness as a team. As one teacher shared privately with Toni, when their administrator wasn't present during their PLC, teachers would sit in the same room but work independently, tackling items on their individual to-do lists; this might be a useful prep, but it is not a PLC and will not grow the collective efficacy and impact of the team. An effective protocol will also prevent the team from getting stuck admiring the problem by moving the conversation out of data paralysis into action. Last, protocols reduce interpersonal conflict among teams because they hold all individuals accountable to shared working agreements; therefore, if any member of the team attempts to derail the conversation, the team can be brought back on track by referencing either the communication agreements or the step they are on in the protocol. Protocols are easier to manage than personalities.

Fortunately, there are several protocols proven to foster meaningful and productive collaboration among educators that lead to improved student outcomes. There is a plethora of free resources available online offering protocols and best practices for a variety of different types of teams, meetings, and collaborative processes (PLC, MTSS, Student Support Team, PBIS, IEP, etc.). Many of these resources are posted by state departments of education, school districts, and nonprofit education organizations. For example, there are some excellent protocols for PLCs created by the National School Reform Faculty and the National Staff Development Council that are available for free online (see the Additional Resources section). There are also numerous books as well as professional development consultants and companies that provide guidance to schools on building the structures and facilitation skills for effective collaboration.

I have worked with schools as a coach helping teachers develop their own protocols, which can be especially valuable when a teacher is sharing a problem of practice with their team. Exploring a problem of practice involves one or more educators discussing a pain point (e.g., minimal student engagement, behavioral challenges, persistently low academic performance, etc.) with their team and inviting their colleagues to contribute ideas and strategies for ways to address it. Exploring a problem of practice as a team is a vulnerable and growth-producing process. This process breaks down the façade of the "perfect teacher" that we spoke about earlier in the chapter and lays bare the truth of the challenges we face as educators. When teachers co-create protocols, it affords them a greater sense of agency and control during this process, which in turn reduces fear and fosters psychological safety.

Whether selecting, creating, or adapting a protocol for collaboration, it is important to consider the degree to which that protocol will foster psychological safety among members of a team. Here are a few important components of psychologically safe protocols for collaboration:

SAFEGUARDS FOR RESPECTFUL AND PRODUCTIVE COMMUNICATION

As we mentioned in previous chapters, revisiting the norms and communication agreements at the beginning of each meeting or collaboration session helps ensure that communication is respectful, equitable, and invitational. For example, Garmston and Wellman posited seven communication agreements for effective PLCs: pausing, paraphrasing, probing for specificity, putting ideas on the table, paying attention to self and others, presuming positive intentions, and pursuing a balance between advocacy and inquiry.[2] These seven behaviors if regularly practiced foster attentive listening and respectful communication as well as self- and social awareness. They also encourage educators to share ideas, ask questions, and advocate for the needs of their students, all of which are hallmarks of psychological safety. Although these seven agreements are helpful, teams can also create their own agreements.

Although meeting norms and communication agreements might feel artificial, awkward, or imposed at first, it is important to keep in mind that with time and practice, the awkwardness will fade, and the team will see the benefit of having safeguards for respectful and productive engagement. Occasionally there are members of a team who intentionally and repeatedly ignore and undermine communication agreements; I have found that these individuals tend to be the biggest bullies on the team. They want to maintain control over their colleagues, so they resist any mention of norms and communication agreements that might equitably distribute voice and power among the members of their team, even more reason that protocols for collaboration must include communication agreements.

If the collaborative process involves educators giving and receiving feedback, then the protocol should include guidelines for how that feedback is delivered and received to ensure that it is clear, constructive, and understood. The Center for Leadership and Educational Equity's Tuning Protocol, which can be found for free online, includes guidance for educators on achieving a balance between what it refers to as "warm" feedback (e.g., acknowledgments, compliments, positive noticings, etc.) and "cool" feedback (e.g., questions, growth areas, concerns, etc.).[3] Many schools I work with use a protocol for noticings (positive statements regarding strengths and best practices) and wonderings (questions related to concerns and areas of improvement) they use to debrief learning walks and observations. Being overserved by colleagues and/or an administrator is an especially vulnerable experience for teachers, and being able to have a voice in the structure of that process ensures greater psychological safety and can facilitate the acceptance and integration of constructive feedback.

DISTRIBUTED RESPONSIBILITY

Clear roles and responsibilities on a team are essential for shared ownership of the collaborative process. This also ensures that no single person is left having to do most of the work for the team, which can foster resentment and burnout. Common roles and responsibilities during a meeting may include facilitator, timekeeper, notetaker, data navigator, and so on. However, if there are responsibilities (e.g., administering an assessment, data entry, etc.) that need to be carried out prior to or after a meeting, then it is critical for the team to specify the action, deadline, evidence of implementation, person(s) responsible, and when they will check in again as a team on the status of this action. Clarity around roles and shared responsibilities allows for greater shared ownership and accountability among members of the team.

A PROCESS FOR COLLECTIVE INQUIRY

Effective protocols foster collective inquiry informed by timely and relevant data. These protocols include steps for analyzing multiple forms of data (e.g., formative assessments, student work samples, conversations with students, observations of students, etc.) in ways that enable educators to identify students' academic, behavioral, linguistic, and/or social-emotional needs. Having a step-by-step process for data analysis helps teams avoid getting stuck admiring the problem or, as we saw in Toni's school, denying and avoiding challenging realities.

As I've mentioned in previous chapters, the mindset that each student is everyone's student is important for fostering shared ownership of student outcomes and a sense of interdependence among educators. Anytime educators meet to collaborate, they should leave that meeting having learned something that will enable them to better support students. One often neglected outcome of effective collaboration is adult learning. To facilitate student achievement, educators have to engage in ongoing learning. Whether it is learning more about their students, learning about a new strategy, or learning about themselves as teachers, I find that protocols that drive inquiry are the most effective at facilitating adult learning. One of the best ways to do this is by including questions in the protocol that guide the team's conversations. Protocols that facilitate inquiry reduce fear by allowing educators to embrace uncertainty, reflect on their own learning, and challenge ineffective practices and fixed mindsets.

ORIENTATION TOWARD ACTION, INNOVATION, AND EXPERIMENTATION

Challenger safety is realized when educators challenge the status quo by developing and implementing practices that improve student outcomes. Innovation is risky but necessary if we are to meet the evolving needs of our students. Can you think of a time when you taught something, but your students didn't learn it, and you weren't sure what to do about that? Even highly effective educators find themselves knowing their students' learning needs but unsure about how to address them. Fortunately, there are several free resources online, such as John Hattie's Visible Learning MetaX and What Works Clearinghouse, that offer educators insight into evidence-based strategies that are proven to support student learning. There are similar resources that feature evidence-based practices for supporting student's behavioral, social-emotional, mental health, linguistic, and attendance needs (see the Additional Resources section at the end of this book to learn more).

Psychologically safe teams invite educators to experiment by creating new pedagogical strategies or tools and collecting data to assess their impact. If a teacher develops a new strategy that improves student outcomes, then they can share it with colleagues to enhance collective efficacy. For example, the teacher might invite their colleagues to view the strategy in action during a learning walk or record themselves engaged in the new practice and share it with colleagues through a microteaching protocol. However, if the strategy is ineffective, then this can be a true test of the level of psychological safety among a team. After all, innovation is risky and does not guarantee success; even ineffective practices can be valuable learning opportunities. Within a psychologically safe team, even our failures are embraced as opportunities to reflect, refine, and improve our practice.

DECISION-MAKING GUIDELINES

When teams lack challenger safety, decision-making is susceptible to bias, intimidation, and manipulation. Therefore, protocols for collaboration need to have clear guidelines for decision-making that ensure equity of voice and shared ownership. I think it's important to acknowledge that some decisions are made *for* educators that are necessary to ensure compliance with federal, state, local, and/or administrative directives. However, most decisions on how to support students are made *by* educators, individually and collectively. A collective efficacy cycle involves multiple decision points for teams including agreeing upon a common challenge and goal; selecting, designing, implementing, and refining pedagogical strategies; and determining how to assess impact and move forward. Protocols that guide teams in a consensus-based approach to decisions ensure a greater likelihood for equity of voice and shared ownership in the decision-making process.

The Center for Leadership & Educational Equity has an extensive collection of protocols available for free online. One of those protocols, developed by Daniel Baron, guides teams through consensus-based decision-making. This protocol defines consensus as meeting three criteria: "I can live with the decision; I will support my colleagues in implementing the decision; I will do absolutely nothing to impede the implementation of the decision."[4] If a member of a team arrives at these three agreements within themselves, then they are a "yes" vote; if not, then they are a "no," and the team should discuss the potential decision further or develop an alternative.

Some schools I work with as a coach use the Fist to Five method to gauge consensus. When it is time to make a decision, each team member holds up either a fist or up to 5 fingers to communicate their level of agreement with the proposed decision (fist = I oppose; 1 finger = I have significant concerns—let's discuss; 2 fingers = I have reservations but could be persuaded; 3 fingers = I am okay with this decision despite some minor concerns or questions; 4 fingers = I support this decision; 5 fingers = I wholeheartedly support this decision). If any member of the team holds up a fist or only one or two fingers, then the team needs to discuss the decision further because they have not reached consensus.

Collaboration protocols that foster challenger safety help teams address challenges through safeguards for respectful and productive communication; distributed responsibility; a process for collective inquiry; an orientation toward action, experimentation, and innovation; and guidelines for decision-making. Although protocols can reduce fear and interpersonal risk during collaboration, they are not enough to achieve real change. A team can have a psychologically safe discussion and determine ways to address a challenge, but unless their behavior changes, then the results will likely remain the same.

REFLECTION QUESTIONS

1. To what extent does your school have structures and protocols in place that facilitate collaboration among staff?
2. What is something that could be done to improve the collaborative process among you and your colleagues?

INDIVIDUAL AND COLLECTIVE ACCOUNTABILITY

Amy Edmondson, the most widely noted scholar and researcher of psychological safety, has spoken about the need for organizations to balance psychological safety and accountability to achieve results.[5] As I mentioned in the previous chapter, accountability looks and feels different in psychologically safe schools. In psychologically safe schools, accountability is less "I gotcha" and more "I got you." Accountability is practiced through providing support and maintaining responsibility rather than faultfinding and blame.

Having said that, psychologically safe teams can feel uncomfortable at times because colleagues are having authentic conversations about the degree to which they have fulfilled their professional commitments. As mentioned in the previous chapter, accountability conversations often center around the fulfillment of tasks (what we are expected to do), processes (how we are expected to do it), and outcomes (the results we are expected to produce). We also explored how when educators maintain accountability by fulfilling their responsibilities and commitments, they experience a greater sense of trust knowing they depend on each other, which invites more contribution and collaboration. In this chapter, we are going to explore what happens when there are breakdowns in accountability and how they can be addressed through challenger safety. For example, if teachers on a team have agreed to implement a new strategy and only two out of five of them are actually implementing it, then the team needs to discuss that reality rather than avoid it. When teams avoid accountability conversations, their morale, cohesion, and efficacy are diminished.

I was once brought in to coach a school after a series of parent complaints sparked an IEP-compliance audit. The audit revealed that members of the special education department had been copying and pasting outdated data and goals into students' IEPs. Some of the IEPs contained incorrect information that had clearly been copied from other students' IEPs. Not every individual in the department was doing this; however, everyone knew about it and said nothing. In the end, even the hardworking special education teachers who had been creating legitimate IEPs were either put on improvement plans or fired. This is an extreme example, but it shows how breakdowns in accountability not only reduce our effectiveness but can harm students.

Having said this, accountability among colleagues is a complex matter to navigate. No teacher should have to be another teacher's boss. In other words, a teacher should not be responsible for reminding a colleague to do their job. At the same time, the only way that teams can function effectively is for educators to be accountable to themselves, their students, and one another. When accountability breaks down, schools end up with an increasing number of staff doing the bare minimum, whereas the rest of the staff have to work even harder to make up for their underperforming colleagues. Fostering accountability among team members doesn't have to be a painful process. As mentioned earlier, it starts with clear roles and responsibilities and creating action plans that detail next steps, deadline(s), evidence of implementation or impact, person(s) responsible, and scheduled status updates.

One thing that teams can do to increase accountability is to schedule time at the beginning of each meeting to check in on the status of their action plan(s). I find that a simple way to do this is to use the colors from a traffic signal to signify where team members are in the process of completing an action item. For example, let's say a team is checking in to see if everyone has administered and graded a common formative assessment. The team members each say a color to signify where they are at in that process: red = I am stuck and have not started; yellow = I am in the process of completing it and need more time or support; green = I have completed it and I can provide any needed artifact, evidence, or final product. If anyone on the team shares a red or yellow, then the team discusses what might be getting in the way of completing their action plan and how they can support one another in getting it done.

If an individual or an entire team repeatedly fails to fulfill their responsibilities, then an administrator needs to take action. I advise administrators to visit the teams in their buildings *at least* once a quarter to assess the health of those teams by noticing how team members communicate with another (including who shares and who doesn't), the team's use of meeting protocols, and the degree to which team members fulfill tasks and responsibilities. By understanding the four stages of psychological safety (inclusion, learner, contributor, challenger), administrators can identify and address any factors that may be hindering a team's collaborative process.

However, an administrator can offer feedback and support only to a point. When feedback is continually ignored, support is rejected, and the individual makes no effort to improve their performance, an administrator may need to place that staff member on a formal improvement plan or, in some instances, engage Human Resources and terminate employment. To put it simply, when constructive feedback and support are continually disregarded, corrective action is needed. I have found that connected and firm administrators even handle the firing process with empathy and care by simultaneously affirming an individual's strengths while acknowledging that their performance did not fulfill the requirements of their position. Educators feel safer working in a school where they know that their administrator is supportive but also holds staff accountable, and everyone is expected to do their job.

REFLECTION QUESTIONS

1. How do you and your colleagues address breakdowns in accountability when someone fails to fulfill a professional duty or commitment and it affects other members of the team or school community?
2. What is something that you and your colleagues could do to create a greater degree of supportive accountability among one another?

NAVIGATING INTERPERSONAL CONFLICTS

Conflict between colleagues is inevitable. Conflicts can arise from disagreements over tasks, teaching styles, student outcomes, competing priorities, cultural differences, personalities, politics, values, points of view; nearly any dimension of identity or work can become a point of contention. Conflicts are also more likely to occur when educators are stressed, overworked, and experiencing burnout. Interpersonal conflicts among colleagues can have a ripple effect throughout the school. Feuding teachers can derail collaboration, pressure colleagues to take sides, and make the day-to-day experience of work harder for themselves and everyone else. I think to some degree the drama can feel exciting, at least at first, but if interpersonal conflicts worsen over time and proliferate among staff, then they eat away at the heart and soul of the school.

Many books and articles on psychological safety in the workplace focus primarily on the behaviors of leaders and teams within organizations and pay less attention to the dynamics of interpersonal relationships within the workplace. However, from my experience working in schools, interpersonal relationships have a significant impact on how educators collaborate with one another, share resources, and work together to support students. Fortunately, there are practices that we can learn from neuroscience, trauma-informed care, and the social sciences that can help us establish challenger safety by transforming toxic interpersonal conflicts into opportunities for greater empathy, connection, understanding, and forgiveness.

PRACTICE SELF-REGULATION

Many of us, including myself, did not grow up in households where we learned healthy ways to cope with stress and conflict. In fact, if you are like me, then you have your own history of exposure to adverse childhood experiences (ACEs) and toxic stress, which have shaped the way your body and brain respond to stress as an adult. Regulation is the process of calming our brain and body's stress response. By practicing self-regulation, we soothe the brain and body's fight, flight, freeze, or fawn response. As these responses lesson, functioning improves in the prefrontal cortex and regions of the brain that help us communicate and be more cognitively and emotionally flexible. We are less likely to engage in people pleasing, faultfinding, or other behaviors that have us avoid or exacerbate conflict. We are better able to respond to challenges rather than react.

Practicing self-regulation benefits everyone, especially those of us affected by ACEs, trauma, and toxic stress. One way to build your capacity for self-regulation is to notice your triggers and how you feel when you are dysregulated and stressed. The next step is to identify strategies that help you experience a sense of calm presence. When applying this principle to navigating interpersonal conflicts at work, it is helpful to have regulation strategies that you can use prior to, during, and after difficult conversations with colleagues.

SEEK TO UNDERSTAND AND BE UNDERSTOOD

When we build an empathic bridge between ourselves and the person with whom we are experiencing conflict, we are more likely to find a mutually beneficial solution to the problem. This requires that we can communicate in a way that fosters mutual understanding and emotional validation, truly relating to one another, even if we don't share the same perspective on the matter. The more we feel understood while growing in our understanding of the other person, the more connected and safer we feel. And, when we feel safe, we tend to think more clearly and creatively, which is useful when resolving conflict. Fortunately, there are strategies we can use to cultivate a sense of relatedness and connection during difficult conversations.

Self-Regulation Strategies for Navigating Interpersonal Conflicts

Prior to a difficult conversation/ interaction . . .	*During a difficult conversation/ interaction . . .*	*After a difficult conversation/ interaction . . .*
• Schedule the conversation for a time & place. Structure creates safety. • Determine what you could think, say, or do that would help you feel to safe during the conversation. • Allow yourself time and space to feel your feelings. • Journal, reflect, or talk with a friend to help you organize your thoughts. • Self-sooth in healthy ways (e.g., mindfulness, exercise, stretch, spend time in nature, take a bath, etc.). • Prayer, meditation, or other spiritual practices may help. • Give yourself a cognitive distraction (e.g., an activity, task, or source of entertainment that requires your mind to think about something else) to take your mind off of the situation.	• Utilize grounding techniques (e.g., take a deep breath, briefly visualize a close friend/ supportive person, notice your feet on the ground, discreetly carry an object you can touch, etc.). • Pause, notice, & name. Pause before responding. Take a second to mentally notice & name what you are feeling emotionally & physically. • Relax your jaw, neck, & shoulders. • Engage in positive mental self-talk. Think to yourself, "I got this," "I'm safe," etc. • Have a pen & paper. Some people find it helpful to write things down during difficult conversations. • Communicate boundaries & step away if the conversation becomes hostile or unprofessional. • Be mindful of your body language & tone of voice. A calm, grounded tone & demeanor will help both you & the other person stay regulated.	• Notice how you are feeling emotionally & physically after the conversation. • Practice one of your self-soothing strategies and/or spiritual practices. • Practice self-compassion. Accept your feelings without shame or blame. Know that you are not alone. Do something kind for yourself. • Talk to a supportive friend. • Journal to get your thoughts & feelings out on paper. • Establish a physical, communication, and/or relational boundary to protect yourself if the relationship is still unhealthy. • Allow yourself time and space to feel your feelings.

Share Hope

When beginning a difficult conversation with a colleague, it can be helpful to share an intention or hope that you have for the conversation. For example, "My hope is that by having this conversation we can understand one another better." Or "My intention is that we can find ways to collaborate that work better for both of us." Ideally, the intention or hope should be something that would benefit both of you. Ask the other person to share what they hope to come out of the discussion with as well. By sharing hopes and intentions, you and your colleague may even notice gradients of agreement between the two of you, where previously you only saw discord.

Communicate to Connect

Marshall Rosenberg's work on Nonviolent Communication (NVC) is an excellent resource for helping individuals and organizations communicate in ways that foster empathy and connection, especially in times of conflict.[6] According to the principles of NVC, every human action is an attempt to meet a need, and when we approach interactions with a willingness to accept and communicate our own needs as well as hear and respond to the needs of others, we arrive at a richer sense of connection and interdependence. We accomplish this by first avoiding criticism, judgment, evaluation, or blame when we communicate with a colleague. We instead use "I" statements to convey our observations, feelings, needs, and requests.

For example, let's say that Maria and Jaimie are colleagues and responsible for monitoring the hallways at the start of each school day to ensure that students make it to class promptly and safely. However, Jaimie rarely shows up for hallway duty (a breakdown in task accountability). Instead, she uses this time to make copies and prepare for her first-period class. Maria is left to monitor the hallways alone, which creates stress for her and a potentially unsafe situation for students. Maria could confront Jaimie and say, "You never monitor the hallways when you're supposed to. If something bad had happened this morning, students could have easily been hurt. But I guess you don't care. The only thing you seem to care about is yourself." This approach would likely quickly escalate into a full-blown argument. Maria could also avoid Jaimie and stew in quiet resentment and frustration. Then she could try to assassinate Jaimie's character by telling the other teachers how self-centered and irresponsible she thinks Jaimie is. This would serve to make other staff members uncomfortable and potentially spark division.

Or Maria could employ the principles of NVC and approach the situation by saying, "When I noticed that I was monitoring the hallway by myself this morning, I felt overwhelmed and anxious because I need our students to be safe. Also, I value our partnership. Would you be willing to monitor the hallways with me in the mornings?" This approach allows Maria to communicate her feelings and needs while making a specific request, which none of the other approaches accomplished. Jaimie will likely feel less defensive and now has an opportunity to respond to Maria's request. Should Jaimie choose to ignore Maria and continue to neglect her hallway duty, Maria may decide to address the concern with the school administrator. However, by first attempting to resolve the issue directly and collegially, her behavior is less likely to be perceived as tattle-telling, snitching, or instigating drama. Also, Maria can feel proud of herself for courageously acknowledging and advocating for her needs.

One caveat before we proceed, the principles and tools of NVC are not a solution to every problem. For example, they may not be useful in addressing abusive workplace dynamics (e.g., threats or acts of harm, harassment, discrimination, etc.) when communication with an aggressor could expose an individual to further harm or manipulation. Behaviors that violate professional codes of conduct are best addressed through Human Resources and/or legal recourse. Fortunately, most forms of conflict in the workplace do not involve abuse; they're uncomfortable and frustrating. NVC can help individuals navigate these conflicts in healthy and productive ways. When we practice NVC in our relationships, we communicate in ways that are clear, respectful, and authentic and more likely to be received by the other person.

The Nonviolent Communication Process

Nonviolent Communication consists of expressing, listening for, and responding to observations, feelings, needs, and requests without criticism, judgment, or blame.

- **Observations**: What we see, hear, imagine, or remember that does not support our well-being
- **Feelings**: The emotions (not the thoughts) that we feel in response to what we observe (e.g., happy, angry, afraid, thankful, etc.)
- **Needs**: What we need and/or value that contributes to our feelings (e.g., safety, belonging, creativity, empathy, love, etc.)
- **Requests**: Specific actions that we would like to have happen (requests are invitations, not demands)

For example, "When I noticed *observation*, I felt *feeling* because I have a need for *need*. Would you be willing to *request*?"

Be Curious

Many times, we don't fully understand the other person's experience of us or their perspective on the situation. The only way we can gain that understanding is by asking open-ended questions and being receptive to the other person's observations, feelings, needs, and requests. This requires us to set aside defensiveness, criticism, judgment, and blame, which requires considerable self-regulation and is easier said than done. However, if we can make the effort to understand the other individual, they are more likely to consider our perspective as well. To accomplish this, we must ask open-ended questions and listen attentively and reflectively.

Actively and Reflectively Listen

When we actively listen, our verbal and nonverbal communication lets the person know that we are paying attention to them and hearing what they are sharing. Active listening requires us to set aside devices such as our cell phone and laptop that might distract us from the other person. Our body language, facial expressions, and eye contact convey that we are attentive to the other person and open to what they have to share. Last, as we listen, it can be helpful to pause before responding and paraphrase what the other person shared. The simple act of paraphrasing, without adding our own judgments or evaluations, lets the person know that they are heard and understood. If you listen for and acknowledge the other person's observations, feelings, needs, and requests, then the two of you may come up with a creative solution that benefits both of you, arriving at a win-win outcome.

If All Else Fails, Disagree and Commit

Ideally, when we reason through a conflict with someone, we arrive at a mutual understanding, compromise, or win-win solution. However, sometimes the only resolution that can be achieved is to commit to a truce by clearly articulating and upholding boundaries to prevent further discord and ceasing behaviors that interfere with either party's professional duties. This process may need to be facilitated through third-party mediation, which we will explore later in this chapter. Although this outcome is less than ideal, it is better than continuing to enact a bitter feud.

REFLECTION QUESTIONS

1. Which one of the following conflict resolution practices do you find the most helpful: practicing self-regulation, sharing hope, NVC, asking open-ended questions, listening attentively and reflectively, seeking a win-win solution, or disagreeing and committing to a truce? How could you apply this practice?
2. Have you ever experienced an interpersonal conflict that was addressed or resolved in a way that improved your relationship with the other person? What did you and the other person say and do (or *not* say and *not* do) that enabled this conflict to become a beneficial experience?

TRANSFORM THE DRAMA TRIANGLE

In the 1960s, Dr. Stephen Karpman proposed his Triangle of Transactional Analysis, more commonly known as the Drama Triangle, to refer to a dysfunctional communication dynamic that enables a persistent and sustained state of conflict among individuals.[7] The Drama Triangle is still used today in therapeutic contexts to help people identify, address, and recover from dysfunctional relational dynamics. To be clear, the Drama Triangle does not apply to circumstances in which an individual has been legitimately harmed by another person and is seeking justice. The Drama Triangle refers to an ongoing process of manipulation, one that is often divorced in some way from reality.

In the Drama Triangle there are three roles: victim, persecutor, and rescuer. The victim convinces themselves and others that they are being harmed, persecuted, or punished unfairly and that they are powerless to do anything about it. The persecutor behaves in ways that are faultfinding, challenging, or superior; however, if they are criticized for acting this way, they may in turn become defensive and try to play the victim role. Last, there is the rescuer. The rescuer rushes to aid the victim, often at the expense their own boundaries and needs. If the rescuer does not to help the victim, they will likely feel guilty. The victim may also feel abandoned and claim that the rescuer's indifference is yet another perpetration against them. The thing to keep in mind about the Drama Triangle is that individuals can switch roles at any time; it is truly a game of manipulation.

I have seen the Drama Triangle play out in schools among staff, students, and parents and guardians. For example, let's say that Ms. Frazer has a student who displays challenging and disruptive behaviors. She claims that she has tried everything to support this student; however, nothing has worked. She wants the student to be placed in a behavior program or at the least be assigned a one-on-one paraprofessional. In reality, Ms. Frazer has in no way differentiated her classroom management to address the behavioral needs of this student. In fact, she often "pokes the bear" and instigates power struggles with the student and then sends him to the office. The principal, Mrs. Henderson, is aware of this and continues to recommend strategies for Ms. Frazer to implement in her classroom. However, Ms. Frazer ignores these suggestions.

Ms. Frazer frequently vents to her grade-level team, crying at times about her frustration with the principal for failing to support her and hold this student accountable for his behavior. She intentionally withheld information from her team about the principal's recommendations as well as the times that she instigated the student's behavior. Mrs. Morris, one of the teachers on Ms. Frazer's grade-level team, is moved by pity for Ms. Frazer, so she contacts the director of student services at the school district, demanding that the student be evaluated for the district's behavior program and that someone at the district office do something about their negligent principal.

In this scenario, Ms. Frazer has positioned herself as the victim of two persecutors (the student and the principal) and successfully recruited Mrs. Morris to act as her rescuer. This is only the current iteration of the Drama Triangle. It is not uncommon in situations like this for the person in Ms. Frazer's position to find herself in the midst of multiple dynamics such as this throughout the school year. I have worked in schools where some staff members embroil several people in the Drama Triangle by pressuring colleagues to choose sides.

David Emerald developed The Empowerment Dynamic to help people escape the harmful Drama Triangle. David Emerald sought to restore power and dignity to each person involved in the conflict. The Empowerment Dynamic transforms the three roles of the Drama Triangle into creator, challenger, and coach.[8] Rather than a victim,

Emerald sees the person who is confronting the challenge as a creator who has a say in how they will choose to respond to the difficult situation. As a creator, they can also choose to view the person they are having difficulty with as a catalyst for their personal growth rather than a persecutor or villain. Rather than playing the role of rescuer, he invites a person who might typically rush to fix or rescue someone to act more like a coach. A coach honors the power and agency of the creator by asking questions that help the creator gain clarity and determine how they will move forward. Coaches provide support, but they do not enable other people's negative or disempowering behaviors. Coaches rarely do something for someone else that that person can do for themselves. In certain circumstances, a coach may decide that the most appropriate response is to offer compassion to someone while allowing that person to accept responsibility for their behavior and experience the consequences of their actions. This might feel uncomfortable for people who are accustomed to people pleasing and rescuing; however, behaving as a coach affirms their boundaries while respecting the other person's autonomy and innate resilience. Last, Emerald reframed the role of persecutor as challenger. The challenger's words and actions present the creator with an opportunity to learn and grow. In The Empowerment Dynamic, the behavior of the challenger can be positive and inspiring. For example, a challenger may express high expectations, provide encouragement, and hold people accountable, presenting a positive impetus for growth.

For example, if we were to reframe the scenario with Ms. Frazer, Mrs. Henderson, and Mrs. Morris through the lens of The Empowerment Triangle we would find a different outcome. For starters, if Ms. Frazer chose to view herself as a creator and the difficult student as a challenger, she might view his disruptive behavior as sign that she needed to try different strategies to support him. If Mrs. Henderson or Mrs. Morris had chosen to view themselves as coaches, they may have asked Ms. Frazer questions about the student and his behavior and how she could respond to it. What need(s) might his behavior be conveying? What could she do proactively and responsively to address that(those) need(s)? Is there anything she should stop doing because it seems to make his behavior worse? By taking on the role of coach, rather than persecutor and rescuer, Mrs. Henderson and Mrs. Morris could have empowered Ms. Frazer to become a better teacher for this young man. Last, there is one other alternative way that The Empowerment Dynamic could be applied to this situation. Mrs. Henderson could choose to occupy the role of challenger. Rather than asking questions and allowing Ms. Frazer to determine her own course of action like a coach would do, Mrs. Henderson could state the strategies that she wishes to see Ms. Frazer implement, offer encouragement, and check in to ensure that the strategies are being implemented. This too would help to disrupt the Drama Triangle and ensure that the Ms. Frazer and the student are supported.

I invite you to look for ways the Drama Triangle may be showing up in your school. If you find yourself in the role of victim, persecutor, or rescuer, how could you change your approach to be more empowering?

Finding Freedom From the Drama Triangle

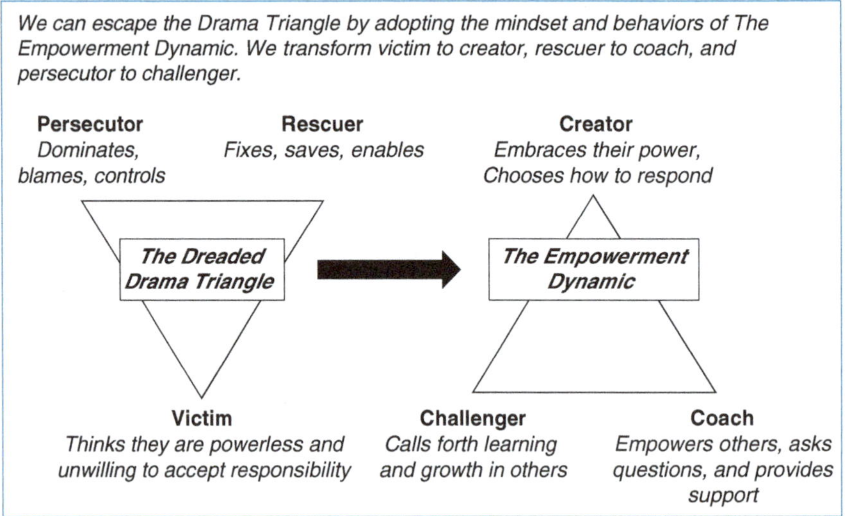

REFLECTION QUESTIONS

1. Given what we know about Ms. Frazer's behavior, do you think her principal should respond to her as a coach (e.g., ask questions, brainstorm solutions, offer support) or as a challenger (e.g., state expectations, provide encouragement and accountability)? Why?
2. Have you ever been involved in the Drama Triangle at work? If so, which role(s) did you play? If you were to apply your insights from The Empowerment Dynamic to this situation, how would your behavior change?

SEEK THIRD-PARTY MEDIATION

Some conflicts escalate and persist until the only hope for resolution is for those involved to engage a neutral third-party to facilitate a resolution. For example, I know a principal who is trained in restorative practices who facilitates restorative conversations and restorative circles among staff. Members of her staff know that they can come to her if they are experiencing difficulties working with a colleague or if their teamwork is hindered by interpersonal conflicts. She meets with each party individually and gathers information from them using the restorative questions (commonly referred to as pre-conferencing), then she brings the parties together and uses those same questions to facilitate a restorative conversation and determine a course of action. The restorative questions provide a protocol for understanding the impact of harmful behaviors on people and relationships while giving everyone involved a voice in determining how matters can be repaired.

Restorative Questions

Questions for the person(s) who engaged in the challenging behavior . . .	Questions for the person(s) negatively affected by the challenging behavior . . .
• What happened? • What were you thinking of at the time? • What have you thought about since? • Who has been affected by what you have done? • In what way have they been affected? • What do you think you need to do to make things right?	• What did you think when you realized what had happened? • What impact has this incident had on you and others? • What has been the hardest thing for you? • What do you think needs to happen to make things right?

These questions may need to be modified to address long-standing patterns of interpersonal conflict in which both parties have engaged in negative behaviors toward one another. Fortunately, there are excellent books, online resources, and professional development trainings available to help individuals learn how to skillfully facilitate restorative conversations. The goal of the restorative process is for the parties involved to determine the actions that will be taken to repair the harm that has occurred and prevent it from happening again. It is best for those involved to document the agreed-upon course of action and establish a plan for how and when they will follow up to ensure that it has been fulfilled.

Again, I want to note that in instances when a colleague's behavior violates the professional code of conduct, especially if they behave in ways that are sexually inappropriate, discriminatory, and/or threatening, then it is imperative to report the incident to your administrator and/or Human Resources and take any other necessary actions to keep yourself safe.

ACCEPT RESPONSIBILITY IF YOU ARE THE "OTHER TEACHER"

In Chapter 1, I mentioned a teacher who was working in a school that was run by cliques and rife with workplace bullying behaviors. You may recall, she said to me, "The hardest thing about teaching isn't the students; it's the other teachers." There are times in my career as an educator when I have been one of the "other teachers," times when I have spread gossip, excessively criticized a colleague, or behaved in ways that were arrogant, self-righteous, and passive aggressive. There are also times when I have failed to follow through on promises and commitments that diminished the trust my colleagues placed in me and hindered our effectiveness as a team.

When I was a classroom teacher, I used to teach my students three steps for accepting responsibility when their words or actions negatively affected others. The three steps I taught them for accepting responsibility were apologize, acknowledge, and repair. These three steps involve offering a sincere apology, acknowledging the impact of your behavior on others, and taking action to repair the harm caused by your behavior and prevent it from happening again.

There have been many times when I have had to utilize the three steps to repair relationships with colleagues. I have apologized for failing to follow through on a commitment or behaving in a way that was hurtful. I've had to acknowledge the affect my actions had on others, which may range from letting them down to adding stress and more work to their plate. And, I've had to take action to repair the situation and commit to changing my behavior moving forward. At times it has been as simple as saying, "I'm sorry I showed up late to this meeting. I know it can be frustrating to have to wait, and I want you to know that I respect your time. I will make sure to arrive on time in the future." Other times, the issues are more complex, and the three steps have sparked a deeper conversation about ways my relationship with my colleague can improve.

I was once advised to change these three steps by someone who said that instead of apologizing, I should thank the other person who has been negatively affected by my behavior. For example, instead of saying, "I'm sorry for being late," I should say, "Thank you for your patience." It seemed like a good idea at first, and I tried it a few times until one day, a friend of mine who is often late for things was so late meeting me at a restaurant for dinner that we lost our reservation, and the restaurant wouldn't seat us. When the first thing she said to me was, "Thank you for being so patient and flexible," I said, "I'm not feeling patient or flexible. I feel frustrated and upset." I realized then that preemptively thanking someone, in place of an earnest apology, can feel like a manipulative attempt to coerce that person into feeling and behaving the way you want them too. Similarly, apologizing insincerely and continuing to engage in the problematic behavior also erodes trust and harms relationships. Before I apologize, acknowledge, or repair, I check in with myself to make sure that I mean it because my integrity and self-respect are on the line in addition to the health of the relationship. Also, I have found that it feels more natural and appropriate to thank someone after I've apologized, especially because their willingness to accept my apology is a gracious act on their part.

Teaching demands all of our humanity, and sometimes we can behave in ways that are less than humane. Accepting responsibility and taking action to repair harm by changing our behavior is a healing balm. If you find yourself in a situation where you need to accept responsibility or want to offer that grace to someone else, I highly encourage it.

FORGIVENESS, BOUNDARIES, AND WELL-BEING AT WORK

Should you receive an apology from a colleague, it is your decision as to whether you accept it. Accepting an apology can open the door to reconciliation and forgiveness. When we forgive, we are not condoning the harmful behavior, we are letting go of the resentment we hold toward the person who committed the wrong. Some people are reluctant to forgive because the resentment they feel provides them a sense of safety. They fear that by forgiving someone, they will set themselves up to be hurt or disappointed again. However, by not forgiving, the anger and resentment they feel may cause them more harm than the other person's behavior did. Holding a grudge has been shown to negatively affect mental and physical health, including increasing the likelihood of developing stress-related illnesses.[9] I have found that when I pair forgiveness with healthy boundaries, I'm able to keep myself safe while granting the other person the opportunity to earn back my trust.

Research on forgiveness in the workplace has explored the willingness of employees to forgive their colleagues for minor workplace transgressions and the affect this has on their job performance as well as their mental and physical health. Forgiveness in the workplace has been linked to heightened productivity, positive mental and emotional states, fewer sick days, less work-related stress, and a reduction in stress-related physical ailments such as headaches.[10] Ultimately, forgiveness is a gift we give ourselves. When we forgive, we release negative emotions in support of our own well-being.

REFLECTION QUESTIONS

1. Reflect on a conflict that has occurred among staff members at your school. Were the parties involved able to arrive at a resolution, compromise, or win-win solution? Why or why not?
2. Is there anyone at work who it would be helpful for you to apologize to? If so, how has your behavior affected this person? What could you do to repair the relationship?

KEY TAKEAWAYS

- Challenger safety in schools encompasses the ways that educators challenge the status quo, engage in productive collaboration, maintain and restore individual and collective accountability, and navigate interpersonal conflict.
- Challenger safety is the pinnacle of psychological safety because challenging the status quo and navigating conflict pose significant interpersonal and professional risks.

- Fear-based school leaders maintain accountability in counterproductive and sometimes harmful ways by engaging in fight, flight, freeze, and/or fawn behaviors.
- Connected and firm school leaders provide a balance of support and accountability.
- Effective collaboration requires educators to embrace the productive struggle inherent in collective efficacy.
- Collaboration protocols that foster challenger safety help teams address challenges through safeguards for respectful and productive communication; distributed responsibility; a process for collective inquiry; an orientation toward action, experimentation, and innovation; and guidelines for decision-making.
- Interpersonal conflicts among colleagues can derail collaboration and erode staff morale.
- When navigating interpersonal conflicts, it is helpful to share hopes and intentions; practice self-regulation strategies; acknowledge and express observations, feelings, needs, and specific requests; seek to understand; listen attentively and reflectively; and work toward a mutually beneficial outcome.
- If an interpersonal conflict cannot be resolved through mutual understanding, compromise, or a win-win solution, the parties involved may wish to seek third-party mediation to assist in establishing boundaries and workable arrangements.
- The Drama Triangle is an unhealthy communication dynamic that perpetuates conflict. Individuals can find freedom from the drama triangle by adopting practices from The Empowerment Dynamic.
- Restorative practices can help administrators and educators resolve conflict and restore relationships.
- Accepting responsibility for negative behaviors and taking action to repair the harm they caused can have a positive impact on interpersonal relationships and workplace culture.

PRACTICES, STRATEGIES, AND TOOLS

Individual Educator
• If you find yourself ensnared in a Drama Triangle, find freedom and agency through The Empowerment Dynamic. Adopt the mindset and behavior of a creator, challenger, or coach. • Navigate interpersonal conflicts by practicing self-regulation, sharing hope, using NVC, seeking to understand, and working toward mutual understanding or a win-win solution. • Question your comfort zone. Consider alternative viewpoints, strategies, and practices. • Voice concerns about practices that are ineffective or harmful. Be courageous in offering alternatives, new ideas, and potential solutions. • If needed, seek third-party mediation to assist in resolving conflicts. • Maintain personal accountability by fulfilling professional duties and commitments. • Acknowledge when you fail to fulfill professional responsibilities in ways that negatively affect others and take action to remedy the situation. • Accept responsibility for harmful behaviors. You may wish to apologize, acknowledge the impact of your behavior, and take action to repair the relationship.
Team
• Implement collaboration protocols that foster psychological safety and collective efficacy. • Embrace productive struggle by acknowledging challenges, setting goals, researching and implementing strategies, collecting and analyzing evidence of impact, refining practices, and celebrating progress. • Maintain collective accountability by developing, following through, and following up on individual professional responsibilities and team action plans. Offer encouragement and support to one another along the way Avoid admiring the problem. Move into action. Research and implement evidence-based strategies, experiment, and innovate. • If a team conversation begins to sound like an echo chamber or a venting session, ask, "Is there another way we can think about this?" or "What *can* we do to address this?" • Utilize The Empowerment Dynamic to avoid the Drama Triangle. • Propose a "same action, same results" scenario to move your team beyond the status quo. For example, "If we keep doing what we've been doing to teach reading comprehension, we're going to get the same results. Is there anything else we could try?" • Practice healthy disagreement by allowing space for multiple perspectives and practicing NVC. • If needed, seek third-party mediation to address interpersonal conflicts that are impeding collaboration.

Administrator
• Learn more about restorative practices and ways they can facilitate conflict resolution and repair harm. • Avoid the Drama Triangle by embracing The Empowerment Dynamic. Adopt the mindset and behavior of a creator, challenger, or coach. • Accept responsibility for harmful behaviors. You may wish to apologize, acknowledge the impact of your behavior, and take action to repair the relationship. • Maintain accountability though connected and firm leadership behaviors. Build positive relationships, give constructive feedback, offer support and encouragement. Engage in corrective action when needed. • Navigate interpersonal conflicts by practicing self-regulation, sharing hope, using NVC, seeking to understand, and working toward a mutual understanding or a win-win solution. • Work with staff to adopt and implement protocols that foster effective collaboration and collective efficacy. • Observe teams as they collaborate. Consider their level of psychological safety (inclusion, learner, contributor, and challenger). Provide support, guidance, and accountability as needed. • Use the Educator Psychological Safety Assessment in Chapter 1 to create an anonymous survey. Have members of each PLC or grade-level or department team complete the survey. Then work with teams to identify steps they can take to foster greater psychological safety. • Invite feedback from staff on ways to improve school-wide practices and systems. What's working? What's not working? What's missing? These three simple questions can uncover opportunities for improvement and innovation.

8

WHERE DO WE BEGIN?

The most common question I receive from educators after they learn about psychological safety is, "Where do we begin?" As a coach, I engage with educators from across the country who work in schools with wildly different workplace cultures, from highly supportive to toxic and hostile. These educators have one thing in common: they all see how their schools could become more psychologically safe spaces for staff, students, and families. They are eager to embark on the cultural work of psychological safety; however, they are unsure of where to begin.

You may be the only staff person in your school aware of the principles of psychologically safety, or you may be a member of a team or part of a school-wide initiative to improve school culture and collective efficacy. An individual staff member, a team, or an entire school staff have different starting points and spheres of influence in this work; however, each of them plays a valuable role in creating a psychologically safe school.

For example, an individual staff member might start by choosing one or two of the practices that we've covered in previous chapters and put them into practice to build more positive relationships with colleagues. A team might start by developing communication agreements and determining ways to improve their meeting protocols. Meanwhile, a school leader and their staff might begin by using this book as a book study and then take the Educator Psychologically Safety Assessment in Chapter 1; this way, they have a sense of the present state of psychological safety within their school as well as structures and practices they can put into place to create a healthier school culture.

Fortunately, whether you are a teacher reading this on your own or an entire school staff engaged in a book study, there are meaningful ways that you can contribute to a psychologically safe work environment. Let's explore some ways that a teacher, team, and school can begin creating a psychologically safe work environment by putting into practice the concepts and strategies we have covered in this book.

IT STARTS WITH ONE

Carlos was a middle school science teacher who was inspired to improve the culture of his department after learning about the concept of psychological safety. The stages of psychological safety gave him a language to describe how he and his colleagues could collaborate more effectively. He volunteered to become the facilitator for his department's team meetings and intentionally integrated psychologically safe practices into their meetings. Carlos started by guiding them through an activity to develop communication agreements. He also proposed a new protocol for the meetings that the team decided to adopt. The new protocol helped the team identify common challenges and move toward solutions.

Carlos modeled many of the behaviors we discussed in our chapters about inclusion, learner, contributor, and challenger safety. When he facilitated team meetings, he asked questions. He gave people think time. He encouraged sharing. If someone seemed disengaged or exceptionally quiet, he would say, "We haven't heard from you yet, and I'm curious what you're thoughts are about this." He also did things like admitting when he didn't know something and asking for input from his colleagues, inviting them to contribute, and then expressing appreciation for their thoughts and ideas.

Carlos's behavior had an impact on the psychological safety of the team. To be clear, it wasn't an overnight shift, nor was it so dramatic that it seemed like anyone's personality radically changed. Rather, little by little, people on the team started to treat one another with a bit more kindness and respect. They also shared in ways that were more invitational, authentic, and supportive. The shift that Carlos appreciated most was that there was more laughter shared among the team. Carlos's decision to act within his sphere of influence had helped improve his team's ability to collaborate in supporting their students and one another.

KNOWING WHEN TO LEAVE

Elena was a reading specialist at an elementary school for more than a decade. She loved teaching kids how to read, and she loved her students. She didn't love working with her colleagues. In her opinion, they were judgmental, insincere, and cliquish. Over the years, she avoided work-related social gatherings. She stopped investing in relationships with her coworkers. She shared less and less during staff meeting. She made herself small to protect herself from what she perceived to be an unhealthy work environment. Sadly, these self-protective efforts exacerbated her sense of isolation at work.

After attending a professional development session with me about psychological safety, she decided to take the risk of becoming more connected with colleagues. She started to put herself out there more during the workday. She said good morning to people in the hallway. She expressed gratitude to coworkers even for small things that in the past she had overlooked. She had conversations with colleagues for the sole purpose of getting to know them more as people rather than just their professional roles. As a result of her efforts, she built stronger relationships with some of the paraprofessionals and teachers at her school, but for the most part, things got worse.

As Elena became more socially courageous, she also started to advocate for herself and her students. An effort was underway in her school district to ban books that discussed race, racism, human sexuality, and gender. Elena felt that this initiative was biased and dangerous. She joined other educators throughout the district in taking a stand for free speech, inclusion, and literacy by opposing the book ban. Because of their efforts, the proposed book ban was defeated. However, Elena was ostracized by many of her colleagues who supported the ban, including her school's instructional specialist. The instructional specialist violated numerous professional boundaries by excessively criticizing Elena in emails and meetings as well as by making snide remarks to her in the hallways and staff lunchroom. Many of the instructional specialist's comments about Elena were personal attacks about Elena's appearance, personality, level of intelligence, and background as an immigrant. When Elena presented her concerns to the principal, he did nothing. Not only did the principal not do anything, but the other staff members either defended the instructional specialist or said nothing out of fear of becoming her next target.

At the end of the school year, Elena decided to transfer to another school in the district. It wasn't that the staff at her new school held similar values and viewpoints to her own; rather it was that they maintained a higher degree of professionalism and psychological safety. The principal of her new school was not afraid to address conflicts head-on and remind her staff of their shared commitment to teach and care for every child. Within months of working at her new school, Elena built stronger and healthier relationships with colleagues than she ever had at her previous school. She continues to teach and advocate for herself and her students.

Interestingly, Elena views her experience as part of a greater lesson in self-empowerment. She shared, "By being more friendly and appreciative at my old school, I learned that I wasn't the problem. That school really was an unhealthy place to work, and I deserved better." Through her efforts to create a more psychologically safe work environment for herself, Elena claimed her power and her worth. Also, she didn't leave teaching. She could have easily given up on the field of education entirely, but instead, she found a school that honored her worth.

STARTING THIS JOURNEY ON YOUR OWN

If you are like Carlos and Elena in that you want to create a more psychologically safe school, but you are the only person among your colleagues who has this awareness and desire, I offer you three suggestions for getting started on this journey: define your sphere of influence, lead by example, and honor your worth.

Defining your sphere of influence is about knowing where you have the capacity to make a difference. Think about the relationships, teams, and committees that you are part of at work. All of these fall within your sphere of influence, as do your own words and actions. By knowing what we can influence, we can be intentional. Defining your sphere of influence is also about knowing what falls outside of it. For example, you can't control other people's behaviors or the decisions that they make. By knowing what is beyond your sphere of influence, you can establish boundaries, reasonable expectations, and a sense of balance. Fortunately, there is no wrong place within your sphere of influence to begin implementing the practices that we have discussed in this book. For example, Carlos chose to focus on making his department's team meetings more psychologically safe, whereas Elena chose to start with her interpersonal relationships with colleagues and fostering a greater sense of inclusion safety. Think about your sphere of influence and ask yourself, where would you *like* to begin?

Once you have defined your sphere of influence, the next step is to lead by example. You can do this by choosing two to three strategies from the earlier chapters of this book and putting them into practice. I often encourage educators to start with "good morning" and "thank you." These simple expressions of salutation and gratitude have a subtle yet powerful effect on the culture of a school. Some educators have told me that after they started making more of an effort to greet their colleagues at the beginning of each workday, they noticed more about the quality of these relationships. They noticed that some were much stronger than others, and they saw opportunities to build bridges with colleagues who were less connected at work.

I advise educators to express more gratitude at work because "thank you" is an antidote to burnout. Stress is contagious in schools, but so is gratitude. By expressing gratitude to our colleagues, we ease the suffering that is caused by working in a field that often fails to honor the hard work of educators. Beyond "good morning" and "thank you," you can choose your own adventure. Think about a team you are on, and determine which of the four stages of psychological safety it is struggling with the most, then choose a strategy to try. The most important thing to keep in mind as you do this is that this work starts from within and is the most impactful when we model the change we want to see.

Psychological safety is not built through people pleasing or superficial "niceness"; it is cultivated through mutual respect. Despite what has been said about the critical role that psychological safety plays in fostering collective efficacy, the most important reason for creating a psychologically safe work environment is that you are worth it. You deserve to work in a school where you feel included, appreciated, supported, and inspired as an educator. Thankfully, you can contribute to creating such a school for yourself and your colleagues. However, as we saw in Elena's story and others like it, there are some school cultures that are toxic and abusive and will require the effort of more than one staff member to substantially improve them. If you work in a school where you are subjected to workplace bullying, harassment, and/or maltreatment, then honoring your worth may mean advocating for your needs or looking for a position in another school. Having said that, I urge you to look for a new position rather than a new career field. Don't give up on the hope, passion, and love that brought you to the field of education or on the promise of young people. There is no such thing as a perfect school. However, if you look, you will likely find a psychologically safe school that will honor your heart and hard work.

FROM ME TO WE

When a team takes on the work of psychological safety, their collective impact is greater than an individual doing this work on their own. I was coaching an elementary school where the fifth grade team was inspired to develop psychological safety. They started by creating communication agreements centered on mutual respect. Each person wrote down what respect meant to them. They gathered everyone's index cards and worked together to draft a list of communication agreements that incorporated everyone's input. This activity was eye-opening for many of the team members because it reflected the personal and varied ways that respect can look, sound, and feel like to other people.

The next step in their journey was to figure out a way to maintain these agreements. They agreed that the agreements needed to be read aloud at the start meetings and posted somewhere where they could be referred to as needed. However, initially, the team could not agree on what to do when one of the agreements was not being adhered to. No one felt comfortable taking on the role of communication steward to support the group. Instead, they came up with a call and response related to their school's mascot (jets) that allowed the whole team to take ownership of maintaining the communication agreements. If an agreement was not being adhered to, then one or more people would say "jets," and the rest of the team would reply "fly back." They found this to be a simple and playful way for them to remind themselves of their agreements.

The team adopted the Center for Leadership & Educational Equity's Tuning Protocol that I mentioned in the chapter on challenger safety to structure their analysis of student work.[1] Through this protocol the team found a greater awareness of their impact and a better understanding of students' learning needs. The team also implemented a protocol for analyzing student assessment data, which helped the team design impactful instruction. By having these protocols in place, their professional learning communities (PLCs) felt like a team effort in which everyone was working together to support all the students in their grade level. This was a dramatic improvement from the past, when their PLCs felt like a room filled with individual teachers each focused solely on their own students. What inspired this team the most about their transformation was that student outcomes improved as their team became more psychologically safe.

Despite their effort and impact, the team had one member who repeatedly resisted the psychological safety journey. Prior to implementing the protocols, this teacher rarely if ever participated during PLCs. When the team adopted their communication agreements, he rolled his eyes anytime they were referenced, even though his input had been included in developing these agreements. When the team introduced the collaboration protocols, he didn't share during the PLC meetings for nearly 2 months. If he was asked to contribute, he'd offer a paltry, insincere response.

It is unrealistic to think that every staff member will see the value of having a more psychologically safe team, even if it leads to improved collaboration and better student outcomes. Some educators will continually place their personal needs and desires above the best interests of their colleagues and their students. Having said that, this team chose to view their reluctant colleague as a challenger, to borrow from Emerald's Empowerment Dynamic, rather than a pain in the you know what. A challenger, as you may recall from the previous chapter, is someone whose behavior requires a more creative response.

Rather than abandoning the protocols or vilifying their colleague, the team moved forward with the work. They expressed appreciation when their colleague contributed during their PLCs. They used humor to take the edge off tough conversations. If he attempted to derail the conversation, which he often tried, especially during action planning, they would simply bring the conversation back on track. They offered support to him and one another when it seemed useful. They made more of an effort to make him feel part of the team, and little by little he started to behave as a team player.

As he felt more included and valued, his behavior shifted. He participated more frequently and began to offer insightful suggestions and propose solutions and strategies. The last time I checked in with the team, the teacher was still resistant to implementing any of the instructional practices from his team's action plans; however, his team members were hopeful that this too may change in the future.

A GAME PLAN FOR TEAMS

When teams begin this work, the first step is to develop the team's knowledge of psychological safety. For example, your team could read an excerpt from this book (Chapter 1 is a good introduction) or an article about psychological safety by Amy Edmonson, Timothy R. Clark, or a similar thought leader (see Additional Resources section). There are also TED Talks, online videos, and podcasts about psychological safety that your team could view or listen to. Regardless of what source(s) of information the team uses to build their understanding, they can then discuss what psychological safety means to them and how it applies to their work as a team.

A wise next step is for a team to explore ways that the structure of their collaborative process could be improved. When a team focuses on the structures and practices that influence collaboration, they avoid getting stuck trying to "fix" the personalities of difficult team members. They can develop these structures by implementing some of the practices that have been discussed in previous chapters (e.g., team-building activities, communication agreements, protocols, etc.). Keep in mind that journey takes time and requires a willingness to experiment, refine, and sustain whichever psychological safety practices are implemented. The goal is for the team to develop a collaborative process that nurtures belonging, learning, appreciation, accountability, and innovation. Fortunately, as the team goes deeper into the work of psychological safety, they also experience its benefits.

Perhaps the most important suggestion I have for a team beginning to work on its psychological safety is to have fun. Find opportunities to get to know one another and connect as human beings. Laugh together. Cry together too, if needed. If a teacher's students make progress, then celebrate it as a win for the entire team. Look for opportunities to celebrate your impact while you continually grow.

HORATIO MIDDLE SCHOOL

Horatio Middle School embarked on their journey toward psychological safety almost by accident in the sense that it wasn't our intention when we started working together. The school had contracted me as a coach to support them in building a multi-tiered system of social-emotional and behavioral supports for their students. Even though the staff expressed a desire to see things improve and acknowledged that their current school discipline system wasn't working, they resisted every strategy or practice that I proposed. When I work with a school that is clearly suffering yet won't take action to address its suffering, the first place I look to intervene is staff well-being. I have developed the opinion, and found it to be true time and again, that when staff are burnt-out and fatigued, they will resist changes that are in their best interests.

With the school leadership team, we administered an Educator Resiliency Needs Assessment like the one found in Chapter 2. We gathered the feedback from the staff, and I reviewed it, highlighting common themes. The needs assessment revealed several widely shared perspectives, including that the school was run by cliques; the leadership team lacked representation from multiple stakeholder groups; there was a lack of clarity and communication about decisions that affected the school community; and many educators witnessed or experienced workplace bullying.

In addition to the needs assessment, we also administered the Educator Psychological Safety Assessment from Chapter 1. We had staff complete the survey anonymously; however, because this was a large school with several different departments, we asked staff to designate their department on the survey. This allowed the leadership team and I to see the varying degrees of psychological safety across departments. It was not surprising to notice that some of the teams with the lowest levels of psychological safety also happened to be some of the lowest-performing teams. For example, the math department had one teacher on the team whose students excelled academically, whereas most of the students in the other teachers' classes performed below standard. Unsurprisingly, this department happened to have one of the lowest levels of psychological safety, revealing a potential root cause for the lack of collective efficacy.

The next phase of the journey was to use the results of the Educator Resiliency Needs Assessment and the Psychological Safety Assessment to inform the development of an action plan. The action plan we developed included school-wide practices that would support each stage of psychological safety. Understanding that this work would take time, we developed a plan that we would implement in phases over the course of 3 years. *Please see Horatio Middle School Psychological Safety Action Plan on the following page.*

As you read through the action plan you, will notice many of the strategies and practices that were covered in previous chapters. A couple things that may stand out to you because they are unique to this school are the decision map and the changes to the leadership team. The needs assessment at Horatio Middle School revealed that most staff perceived the school's leadership team to lack adequate representation. Their perceptions were accurate given that when I started working with the school, the leadership team of this large urban middle school consisted of only four people: the principal, school counselor, instructional specialist, and office manager. As part of our psychological safety work, we dismantled this leadership team and created a new one that included an elected representative from every department as well as the principal, counselor, specialists, office manager, and a paraprofessional. We encouraged new staff as well as those who had worked at the school for a long time to volunteer to represent their department on the leadership team. We were explicit that having a diverse array of perspectives and experience would more accurately represent the whole school.

I worked with this new leadership team to develop a clear sense of their purpose, roles, and responsibilities. This included adopting a consensus-based decision-making model, creating a decision map, and developing a system for gathering staff input as needed. The decision map was created because on the needs assessment staff had said that there was a lack of clarity and communication about decisions. As a result, when a significant decision was made, it was not uncommon for rumors to spread and conflict to develop among staff. The first step in addressing this was to create clarity about who makes which decisions. *Please take a moment to read through the decision map.* You will notice that it outlines the major decisions that staff members and teams in the school make throughout the year. The decision map is not meant to be an exhaustive list, rather a general overview of major decisions, especially decisions where there is often a lack of clarity as to who is responsible within the school.

After we drafted the decision map, we presented it to the staff. We used an anonymous online survey to gather their input about any changes that needed to be made. After it was finalized, we periodically referenced the decision map throughout the school year to spark conversations about how specific decisions were made, the reasoning behind them, and what recourse staff members could take if they wished to express disagreement. The decision map and the messaging about school-wide decisions lessened the dysfunctional communication and conflict that had once been common among the staff.

Horatio Middle School Decision Map

Individual Teacher (based upon commonly held expectations)	Grade-Level and Department Teams	SpEd Team (may collaborate with administration, teachers, students, parents, EAs, & related service providers)
• Classroom management style • Implementation of classroom-based MTSS academic, social-emotional, linguistics, & behavioral supports • Classroom & common areas discipline plan • Standards-aligned, evidence-based supplementary academic materials • Parent communication • Positive classroom culture & teacher–student relationships	• Pacing guide & common planning • Formative & summative unit assessments • Common grading criteria • Common challenge & instructional strategies • Coordinating and progress monitoring MTSS with the assistance of additional staff (e.g., counselor, school psychologist, administrator, etc.) • Planning field Trips	• Developing IEPs • Appropriate instructional and behavioral supports for students with IEPs • Behavior plans for students with disabilities • Implementation & compliance with IEP, BSP, BIP • Determining least restrictive environment for students with IEPs • Contingency & safety plans for students with IEPs • Budget for SpEd
Leadership Team	**Administrator**	**Operations Team**
• Bell schedule* • Calendar** • Academic plan** • Supervision schedule** • Scheduling & accommodations for state testing • School-wide MTSS data analysis & implementation	• School-wide staff/student safety • Staff/student discipline • Final teacher/line assignments • Field trip approvals • Financial plan** • School-wide assembly approvals • Hiring • Assigning teacher in charge • Communications to all-staff, families, & community	• Job-specific decisions that allow for a functional campus

*Teacher Vote **Teacher/Staff Input

I also want to mention one action step that was intentionally left off the action plan. The action plan includes a great deal of supportive accountability: learning walks, collaboration protocols, communication agreements, restorative conversations, and the instructional specialist providing additional support to teams that are struggling with or resisting the psychological safety journey. The item that was left off the action plan was that the needs assessment included multiple complaints about the unprofessional behavior of a specific staff member. This teacher had allegedly violated the school's professional code of conduct by harassing, belittling, and threatening fellow staff members. These behaviors were common knowledge in the school; however, the principal had chosen to ignore them perhaps because she too feared this teacher. I asked the principal to please talk with staff, document their complaints, and contact Human Resources. If these behaviors were allowed to continue, they would erode the work we were doing and cause harm. Thankfully, the principal complied with my request. Ultimately, the teacher was put on an improvement plan until Human Resources concluded their investigation and she was terminated. Several staff members expressed gratitude to the principal for finally taking a stand to uphold professionalism and safety in their school.

Over the course of the next 3 years, I worked with Horatio Middle School in implementing their psychological safety action plan. As is often the case, they needed much less of my support in Year 3 than they did in Year 1. I was heartened by their progress, which was measured both qualitatively and quantitively. Aside from staff feedback, we also administered a Collective Teacher Efficacy Beliefs Scale developed by Tschannen-Moran (see the Additional Resources section at the end of this book for more information) prior to implementing the psychological safety action plan.[2] We re-administered the assessment at the end of Year 1 and saw a dramatic improvement in teachers' collective efficacy beliefs, which was sustained in Years 2 and 3. We also saw a significant improvement in students' academic performance and behavioral outcomes by the end of Year 1 with improved academic outcomes and a reduction in behavioral referrals. By the end of Year 2, the majority of students were achieving over a year's worth of academic growth in a year's time. These findings are evidence of the powerful influence that psychological safety has on collective efficacy.

	Horatio Middle School Psychological Safety Action Plan			
	Inclusion Safety	**Learner Safety**	**Contributor Safety**	**Challenger Safety**
Year 1	Implement staff circles and/or team-building activities quarterly Conduct professional development training on workplace bullying & how to address it	Choose an area of practice to explore each quarter (e.g., relationships, routines, regulation, etc.) and invite educators to share strategies, tools, successes, questions, & problems of practice	Celebrate growth during data meetings (not only proficiency) Develop school-wide communication agreements to use during meetings	Create a decision map Restructure the leadership team to create equity of voice Adopt a consensus-based decision-making model for teams
Year 2	Conduct professional development training on strategies to mitigate burnout & compassion fatigue Continue quarterly staff circles & team-building activities Pair new teachers with buddy teachers	Adopt collaboration protocols for PLCs and collaboration around students' social-emotional and behavioral needs Create structured, low-stakes opportunities for staff to learn from and with each other (e.g., learning walks, microteaching, share strategies, tools, & successes, etc.), including creating a process for giving & receiving constructive feedback School leadership will regularly communicate to staff throughout the year that it is OK to ask for help, make mistakes, propose new ideas, and learn together as we grow	Replace Teacher of the Month with a monthly all-staff appreciation (e.g., coffee & bagels, early dismissal from a meeting, etc.) Monthly staff meetings will begin with a brief turn & talk for staff to reflect on something they are proud of, grateful for, etc. Revisit & maintain communication agreements	Introduce restorative practices (RP) and Nonviolent Communication (NVC) during professional development to equip staff with tools for resolving conflict Present staff with workplace conflict scenarios for staff to apply their learning about RP & NVC Make principal and school counselor available to facilitate restorative conversations between staff, if needed Build the leadership team's capacity gather input from all staff when needed

(Continued)

(Continued)

Year 2 (continued)		Encourage frequent informal classroom visits accompanied with positive feedback and formal observations with a pre- & post-observation meeting intended to foster a learning partnership between administrator & teacher		Implement the communication agreements & collaboration protocols with support from the instructional coach
Year 3	Administer the ProQOL assessment during a staff meeting & discuss self and collective care strategies (2x per year) Continue quarterly staff circles & team-building activities Continue buddy teacher program for new teachers & expand it across all departments for all new staff	Utilize learning walks to strengthen accountability & consistency of the implementation of school-wide social-emotional & behavioral supports Sustain and refine collaboration protocols Continue efforts from the previous 2 years	Revisit and maintain communication agreements, which may include presenting scenarios to staff on how to respond if/when agreements are not adhered to Continue the celebration of progress, all-staff appreciation, etc.	Revisit RP & NVC strategies as needed Administrator & counselor will continue to facilitate restorative conversations among staff as needed Leadership team will continue to identify needs of the staff & take action to address them Instructional coach will continue to support teams as needed

A WHOLE-SCHOOL APPROACH

When the entire school staff engages in this work, it's thrilling because it creates a more psychologically safe environment that benefits educators, students, and families. If an entire school staff is going to embark on this journey, the first thing that they need to do is build their understanding of psychological safety. They might accomplish this through a professional development training, reading an article together, watching an online video, and/or using this book for a book study.

A principal I coached shared a strategy with me that she used when she wanted her whole staff to engage in a book study, but there wasn't enough time to devote to it. Her method can be used with this book as well. Have the staff divide themselves into groups. Assign each group a section of this book. Give them about 30 minutes to read their section. Then have each group write on chart paper or a presentation slide a brief synopsis and key takeaways in concise bullet points. Then, have the groups come to together and present on their section in the order that it occurs in the book. Each group's presentation should be only about 5 minutes. If you use this method, the staff will have completed their entire book study in approximately 90 minutes to 2 hours and will have acquired a foundational understanding of the stages of psychological safety.

A next step is to assess where the school currently is in terms of psychological safety. A school can achieve this by having all staff members complete the Educator Psychological Safety Assessment (found in Chapter 1) anonymously. Some large schools that I work with have had teachers identify their grade level or department when completing the assessment, while their identity remains anonymous. Being able to disaggregate the data in this way can be helpful for schools that have a large staff because each grade level or department can have its own culture.

I encourage school leadership teams to present the results of the Educator Psychological Safety Assessment to the entire staff. The results of the assessment allow the staff to better understand their school's unique strengths and growth areas. However, I don't encourage leadership teams to share the results disaggregated by grade level or department. It is common for some teams in the same school to have dramatically lower levels of psychological safety than others. Although this information is helpful to the leadership team because it lets them know which teams are going to need more support in their journey toward psychological safety, displaying the results by grade level or department team can run the risk of further fracturing teams with low levels of psychological safety and cause other teams to view them disparagingly. Therefore, I encourage sharing an overview of the results with the entire school staff but not breaking the results down by grade level or department.

The next phase in the journey is for the staff to develop an action plan for how their school will become more psychologically safe. I recommend using an action planning template that invites the leadership team to identify school-wide practices to implement that address each stage of psychological safety, as you can see in Horatio Middle School's action plan. It is important to keep in my mind that culture work takes time, so any action plan that the team develops should consider at least the following 2–3 school years with an understanding that the plan can be revisited and modified as needed.

As we saw in the example Horatio Middle School, administering the Educator Resiliency Needs Assessment (found in Chapter 2) can be part of the action planning process. The data from the needs assessment can help the leadership team determine which practices will more effectively address the needs of the staff. However, this process is more complicated and may require the school to enlist an external coach or consultant to assist in this process. The benefit of creating a psychological safety action plan that arises from the needs of the staff is that it is more likely to alleviate burnout and cultivate staff well-being, resilience, and efficacy.

Once an action plan has been drafted, it is important for the leadership team to share the action plan with the staff, explain the reasoning behind it, and gather the staff's feedback regarding any necessary modifications. Then it is time to begin implementation. This is when the real journey begins!

A CALL TO ACTION

I am writing this at a time when it is evident that our education system must change. Our students are suffering, and they are showing this through their behavior and mental health. Our educators are suffering more. They are leaving the field at a staggering pace because it has failed to support and sustain them. Psychologically safety builds relationships that are strong enough to tackle huge challenges. If we are to transform our education system, secure the compensation that teachers deserve, advocate for the resources our schools need, and create the learning environments that we and our students deserve, then we need each other.

Psychological safety enables us to work together in ways that reduce fear and suffering. Many educators are subjected to the trauma of working in schools that are under-resourced and physically and emotionally unsafe. That pain can easily be weaponized against the self through perfectionism and relentless self-criticism or turned against others in the form workplace bullying and relational aggression. Healing ourselves, our schools, and our education system starts with establishing a sense of safety.

Welcome to the threshold of your journey toward a psychologically safe school. I hope that you will continue to use this book as a resource. Allow the concepts and stories we have explored to inspire your heart and mind. Decide what concepts and strategies you will take from this book and put them into practice. Take time periodically to notice the positive changes they inspire within you and within your relationships. Honor yourself by being the change you wish to see in your school.

REFLECTION QUESTIONS

1. Define your sphere of influence. What are the teams, roles, systems, and relationships that you have the capacity to influence within your school?
2. What actions can you take within your sphere of influence to create a more psychologically safe school for you and your colleagues? How will you tell if your actions are making a difference?

KEY TAKEAWAYS

- An individual staff member, a team, or an entire school staff have different starting points and spheres of influence in this work; however, each of them plays a valuable role in creating a psychologically safe school.

(Continued)

(Continued)

- An individual educator can begin their psychological safety journey in their school by defining their sphere of influence, leading by example, and honoring their worth.
- School teams can begin their psychological safety journey by building their knowledge of the stages of psychological safety, implementing protocols that facilitate effective collaboration, and finding fun and meaningful ways for team members to connect with one another.
- A whole-staff approach to psychological safety begins with the staff building their knowledge of the stages of psychological safety, assessing the level of psychological safety within their school, and developing and implementing an action plan that is informed by staff input and addresses each stage of psychological safety.
- Psychological safety builds relationships that are strong enough to transform schools.

PRACTICES, STRATEGIES, AND TOOLS

Individual Educator
• Define your sphere of influence: the roles, teams, systems, and relationships that you influence. • Lead by example. Engage in behaviors that cultivate inclusion, learner, contributor, and challenger safety. • Honor the difference that you make. Notice the positive impact that your efforts to create a more psychologically safe school have on you and others. • Treat yourself. Culture work can be hard; make time for things you enjoy.
Team
• Develop your knowledge of psychological safety as a team. • Adopt and implement protocols for effective collaboration. • Notice how collaboration and relationships improve as team members experience greater trust and psychological safety. • Find fun and meaningful ways to build and maintain relationships as a team. Connect from the heart when doing hard work.
Administrator
• Build the staff's knowledge of psychological safety through professional development, book study, or other resources. • Lead by example. Engage in behaviors that cultivate inclusion, learner, contributor, and challenger safety. • Administer the Educator Psychological Safety Assessment anonymously to determine the degree of psychological safety among staff in your school. • Work with your leadership team to develop and implement a school-wide Psychological Safety Action Plan. The action plan should include strategies and practices that foster each stage of psychological safety • You may wish to utilize additional tools to guide and assess the impact of your psychological safety work, such as the Educator Resiliency Needs Assessment and a collective efficacy assessment. • Honor yourself! Your commitment to psychological safety makes you a courageous and transformational leader!

EDUCATOR PSYCHOLOGICAL SAFETY ASSESSMENT

Directions: Please read the following statements and decide how strongly you agree or disagree with each statement on a scale ranging from (1) "Strongly Disagree" to (5) "Strongly Agree."

	Strongly Disagree 1	*Disagree 2*	*Neutral 3*	*Agree 4*	*Strongly Agree 5*
1. Staff members within my school can bring up problems, challenges, and tough issues.					
2. I feel safe enough to try new strategies within my school.					
3. It is difficult to ask other staff members at my school for help.					
4. I feel safe expressing my ideas, questions, and concerns at work.					
5. None of my colleagues would intentionally undermine my efforts.					
6. At my school, my unique skills and talents are recognized, valued, and utilized.					

(Continued)

(Continued)

	Strongly Disagree 1	*Disagree 2*	*Neutral 3*	*Agree 4*	*Strongly Agree 5*
7. My colleagues and I learn from and with one another.					
8. If I make a mistake at work, it will likely be held against me.					
9. If I share about a success at work, my colleagues will respond positively.					
10. Colleagues within my school sometimes reject others for being different from them.					

Scoring Instructions: To determine the level of psychological safety, add together your ratings for all the statements. Statements 3, 8, and 10 are reverse scored. For these statements you will need to change the score before adding it to your other ratings. For statements 3, 8, and 10 if you chose 1 change it to 5; 2 to 4; 3 to 3; 4 to 2; and 5 to 1.

Calculate Your Score	Range of Scores	Level of Psychological Safety
1. ___ 2. ___ 3. ___ = ___ 4. ___ 5. ___ 6. ___ 7. ___ 8. ___ = ___ 9. ___ 10. ___ = ___ Total: ____	20 or less Between 21 and 39 40 or more	Low Moderate High

ADDITIONAL RESOURCES

PSYCHOLOGICAL SAFETY

The Fearless Organization: Creating Psychological Safety in the Workplace for Learning, Innovation, and Growth by Amy C. Edmondson (John Wiley & Sons Inc.)

The 4 Stages of Psychological Safety: Defining the Path to Inclusion and Innovation by Timothy R. Clark (Barrett-Koehler Publishers)

Building a Psychologically Safe Workplace: TEDx Talk by Amy Edmondson that explores the relationship between psychological safety and accountability. You can access it at https://www.youtube.com/watch?v=LhoLuui9gX8

Achieving Psychological Safety: A brief video by Simon Sinek that speaks to the power of psychologically safe leadership. You can access it at https://www.youtube.com/watch?v=PYZIvlf5ROw

BURNOUT, BOUNDARIES, AND WELL-BEING

ProQOL Measure: A free research-based tool to assess your level of burnout, secondary trauma, and compassion satisfaction. You can access it a: https://proqol.org/proqol-measure

Adverse Childhood Experiences (ACEs) Questionnaire: An online tool to assess your exposure to ACEs. You can access it at https://numberstory.org/assessment/

Building Resilience in Students Impacted by Adverse Childhood Experiences: A Whole Staff Approach by Victoria E. Romero, Ricky Robertson, & Amber N. Warner (Corwin)

Complex PTSD: From Surviving to Thriving by Pete Walker (CreateSpace Independent Publishing)

Self-Compassion: The Proven Power of Being Kind to Yourself by Kristin Neff (William Morrow)

Set Boundaries, Find Peace: A Guide to Reclaiming Yourself by Nedra Glover Tawwab (Tarcher Perigee)

The Dance of Anger: A Woman's Guide to Changing the Patterns of Intimate Relationships by Harriet Lerner (Perennial Currents)

Promoting Mental Health and Well-Being in Schools: An Action Guide for School and District Leaders: A guide developed by the Division of Adolescent and School Health, National Center for Chronic Disease Prevention and Health Promotion, and the Centers for Disease Control and Prevention that can be accessed at https://www.cdc.gov/healthyyouth/mental-health-action-guide/pdf/DASH_MH_Action_Guide_508.pdf

Trauma-Informed Teaching Video Series: An eight-episode video series that explores trauma-informed social-emotional and behavioral strategies and practices. You can access it at https://www.adlit.org/trauma-and-teaching/trauma-informed-teaching-video-series

COLLECTIVE EFFICACY AND IMPACTFUL COLLABORATION

Collective Teacher Efficacy Beliefs Scale: Measures developed by Megan Tschannen-Moran and her colleagues to assess educators' self and collective efficacy beliefs. You can access these tools at https://mxtsch.pages.wm.edu/research-tools/

Collective Efficacy: How Educators' Beliefs Impact Student Learning by Jenni Donohoo (Corwin)

Collective Leader Efficacy: Strengthening Instructional Leadership Teams by Peter DeWitt (Corwin)

Collaborating Through Collective Efficacy Cycles: Ensuring All Students and Teachers Succeed by Toni Faddis, Douglas Fisher, & Nancy Frey (Corwin)

PLC+: Better Decisions and Greater Impact by Design by Douglas Fisher, Nancy Frey, John Almarode, Karen Flories, & Dave Nagel (Corwin)

Tuning Protocol: This collaboration protocol can be accessed at https://www.schoolreforminitiative.org/download/tuning-protocol/

Visible Learning MetaX: An online database that allows educators to explore the impact of hundreds of influences on student achievement based upon the findings of John Hattie's Visible Learning research. You can access it at https://www.visiblelearningmetax.com

What Works Clearinghouse: An online database of evidence-based instructional strategies and approaches. You can access it at https://ies.ed.gov/ncee/wwc/

INCLUSION, BELONGING, AND EQUITY

Collective Equity: A Movement for Creating Communities Where We All Can Breathe by Sonja Hollins-Alexander & Nicole V. Law (Corwin)

Cultural Proficiency: A Manual for School Leaders by Randall B. Lindsey, Kikanza Nuri-Robbins, Raymond D. Terrell, & Delores B. Lindsey (Corwin)
Race Resilience: Achieving Equity Through Self and Systems Transformation by Victoria E. Romero, Amber N. Warner, & Justin Hendrickson (Corwin)

EFFECTIVE COMMUNICATION AND CONFLICT RESOLUTION

Better Conversations: Coaching Ourselves and Each Other to Be More Credible, Caring, and Connected by Jim Knight (Corwin)
Nonviolent Communication: A Language of Life: Life-Changing Tools for Healthy Relationships by Marshall B. Rosenberg (PuddleDancer Press)
The Power of TED The Empowerment Dynamic* by David Emerald (Polaris Publishing)
The Power of Vulnerability: A TED Talk by Brené Brown that can be accessed at: https://www.youtube.com/watch?v=iCvmsMzlF7o

REFERENCES

CHAPTER 1

1. Collective Teacher Efficacy (CTE) according to John Hattie. (2018, March). Visible-Learning. https://visible-learning.org/2018/03/collective-teacher-efficacy-hattie/
2. Rozovsky, J. (2015, November 17). *The five keys to a successful Google team.* Re:Work. https://rework.withgoogle.com/blog/five-keys-to-a-successful-google-team/
3. Edmondson, A. (1999). Psychological safety and learning behavior in work teams. *Administrative Science Quarterly, 44*(2), 350–383.
4. Clark, T. R. (2020). *The 4 stages of psychological safety: Defining the path to inclusion & innovation.* Berrett-Koehler Publishers, Inc.

CHAPTER 2

1. Freudenberger, H., & North, G. (1985). *Women's burnout: How to spot it, how to reverse it, and how to prevent it.* Doubleday.
2. Guise, S. (2019). *Elastic habits: How to create smarter habits that adapt to your day.* Selective Entertainment LLC.
3. Lerner, H. (2014). *The dance of anger: A woman's guide to changing the patterns of intimate relationships.* William Morrow Paperbacks.
4. Substance Abuse and Mental Health Services Administration (SAMHSA), Trauma and Justice Strategic Initiative. (2012). *SAMHSA's working definition of trauma and guidance for trauma-informed approach.* Author.
5. Walker, P. (2013). *Complex PTSD: From surviving to thriving.* Azure Coyote Publishing.

CHAPTER 3

1. Hay, L. (1991). *The power is within you.* Hay House, Inc.
2. Vévoda, J., Vévodová, Š., Nakládalová, M., Grygová, B., Kisvetrová, H., Grochowska Niedworok, E., Chrastina, J., Svobodová, D., Przecsková, P., & Merz, L. (2016). The relationship between psychological safety and burnout among nurses. *Occupational Medicine / Pracovní LéKarství, 68*(1), 68. https://www.researchgate.net/profile/Marie-Nakladalova/publication/305032643_The_relationship_between_psychological_safety_and_burnout_among_nurses/links/60ad3e56458515bfb0a30984/The-relationship-between-psychological-safety-and-burnout-among-nurses.pdf
3. Paul, J. (2023). The role of psychological safety on employee satisfaction and retention in healthcare delivery settings: A systematic literature review. [Capstone Experience, University of Nebraska]. https://digitalcommons.unmc.edu/cgi/viewcontent.cgi?article=1274&context=coph_slce
4. Kim S., Lee H., & Connerton T. P. (2020). How psychological safety affects team performance: Mediating role of efficacy and learning behavior. *Frontiers in Psychology, 11*(1581). https://doi.org/10.3389/fpsyg.2020.01581
5. Newman A., Donohue R., & Eva N. (2017). Psychological safety: A systematic review of the literature. *Human Resources Management Review, 27*(3), 521-535. https://doi.org/10.1016/j.hrmr.2017.01.001
6. Hoogsteen, T. J. (2020). Collective efficacy: Toward a new narrative of its development and role in achievement. *Palgrave Commun, 6*, 2. https://doi.org/10.1057/s41599-019-0381-z
7. Dewitt, P. (2019). How collective teacher efficacy develops. *Educational Leadership, 76*(9). https://www.ascd.org/el/articles/how-collective-teacher-efficacy-develops

CHAPTER 4

1. Rosenberg, M. (2015). *Nonviolent communication: A language of life* (3rd ed.). Puddledance Press.
2. Finkel, E. J., Bail, C. A., Cikara, M., Ditto, P. H., Iyengar, S., Klar, S., Mason, L., McGrath, M. C., Nyhan, B., Rand, D. G., Skitka, L. J., Tucker, J. A., Van Bavel, J. J., Wang, C. S., & Druckman, J. N. (2020). Political sectarianism in America. *Science, 370*(6516), 533-536. https://doi.org/10.1126/science.abe1715
3. Waters, M. (Director). (2004). *Mean girls* [Film].

4. Namie, G. (2021). *2021 WBI U.S. workplace bullying survey.* Workplace Bullying Institute. http://workplacebullying.org/wp-content/uploads/2023/06/2021-Full-Report.pdf

5. Timothy, C. R. (2023, May 16). Stage 1: Inclusion safety. LeaderFactor. https://www.leaderfactor.com/post/stage-1-inclusion-safety#:~:text=Inclusion%20safety%20allows%20us%20to,In%20short%2C%20it%27s%20debilitating

6. Wang, H., Braun, C., & Neck, P. (2017, September). How the brain reacts to social stress (exclusion)-A scoping review. *Neuroscience & Behavioral Reviews, 80,* 80-88. https://doi.org/10.1016/j.neubiorev.2017.05.012

7. Kross, E., Berman, M. G., Mischel, W., Smith, E. E., & Wager, T. D. (2011). Social rejection shares somatosensory representations with physical pain. *Proceedings of the National Academy of Sciences of the United States of America, 108*(15), 6270-6275. https://doi.org/10.1073/pnas.1102693108

CHAPTER 5

1. Clark, T. R. (2020). *The 4 stages of psychological safety: Defining a path to inclusion and innovation.* Berrett-Koehler Publishers.

2. #RSAshorts. (2015, February 3). Brené Brown on Blame [Video]. YouTube. https://www.youtube.com/watch?v=RZWf2_2L2v8

3. Barni, D., Danioni, F., & Benevene, P. (2019). Teachers' self-efficacy: The role of personal values and motivations for teaching. *Frontiers in Psychology, 10*(1645). https://doi.org/10.3389/fpsyg.2019.01645

4. Hoogsteen, T. J. (2020). Collective efficacy: toward a new narrative of its development and role in achievement. *Palgrave Commun 6, 2.* https://doi.org/10.1057/s41599-019-0381-z

5. Dewitt, P. M. (2022). *De-implementation: Creating the space to focus on what works.* Corwin

6. The Center for Victims of Torture. (2009). *Professional Quality of Life Measure (ProQOL 5.0).* https://proqol.org

7. Hicks, T. P., Sullivan, M., Sexton, B., & Adair, K. C. (2019). Transforming culture through resiliency and teamwork. *American Nurse Today, 14*(2), 41-43.

8. Knight, J. (2021, March 2). Data rules. *The instructional coaching blog.* https://www.instructionalcoaching.com/blog/data-rules

9. Archer, J., Cantrell, S., Holtzman, S. L., Joe, J. N., Tocci, C. M., & Wood, J. (2016). *Better feedback for better teaching: A practical guide to*

improving classroom observations. Jossey-Bass. https://usprogram.gatesfoundation.org/-/media/dataimport/resources/pdf/2016/12/betterfeedbackbetterteaching.pdf?rev=babf69d0c7e24e05bd413a662b342d45&hash=19E16CE41549A4627C9E450853C20BD0

CHAPTER 6

1. King, J. E., & Weadé, J. (2022). *Colleges of education: A national portrait* (2nd ed.). American Association of Colleges for Teacher Education.

2. Yan, H. (2018, May 29). *Here's what teachers accomplished with their protests this year.* CNN. https://www.cnn.com/2018/05/29/us/what-teachers-won-and-lost/index.html

3. Allegretto, S. (2022). *The teacher pay penalty has hit a new high: Trends in teacher wages and compensation through 2021*. Economic Policy Institute. https://www.epi.org/publication/teacher-pay-penalty-2022/

4. Remarks to United States Committee on UNICEF. (July 25, 1963). Pub. Papers Chronological File, Box 013, July 1963, 16-31. https://www.jfklibrary.org/asset-viewer/archives/jfkwhcfchron-013-008#?image_identifier=JFKWHCFCHRON-013-008-p0097

5. San Antonio Independent School District v. Rodriguez, 411 U.S. 1 (1973). https://supreme.justia.com/cases/federal/us/411/1/

6. Espinoza v. Montana Department of Revenue, 591 U.S. (2020). https://supreme.justia.com/cases/federal/us/591/18-1195/

7. Clark, T. R. (2020). *The 4 stages of psychological safety: Defining a path to inclusion and innovation*. Berrett-Koehler Publishers.

8. Beheshti, N. (2018, November 20). *Benefits of a year-round attitude of gratitude in the workplace*. Forbes. https://www.forbes.com/sites/nazbeheshti/2018/11/20/benefits-of-a-year-round-attitude-of-gratitude-in-the-workplace/?sh=1732c3f61bc5

9. Allan, S. (2018). *The science of gratitude* [White paper]. Greater Good Science Center at UC Berkeley. https://ggsc.berkeley.edu/images/uploads/GGSC-JTF_White_Paper-Gratitude-FINAL.pdf?_ga=2.51257770.246418475.1638563377-157927757.1638563377

10. Spence, J. R., Brown, D. J., Keeping, L. M., & Lian, H. (2013). Helpful today, but not tomorrow? Feeling grateful as a predictor of daily organizational citizenship behaviors. *Personnel Psychology, 67*(3), 705-738. https://doi.org/10.1111/peps.12051

11. Chan, D. (2010). Gratitude, gratitude intervention and subjective well-being among Chinese school teachers in Hong Kong. *Educational Psychology, 30,* 139-153. https://doi.org/10.1080/01443410903493934

12. Locklear, L. R., Taylor, S. G., & Ambrose, M. L. (2021). How a gratitude intervention influences workplace mistreatment: A multiple mediation model. *Journal of Applied Psychology, 106*(9), 1314-1331. https://doi.org/10.1037/apl0000825

13. Roberts, P. (2018). Three good things: Build resilience and improve well-being. *American Nurse Today, 13*(12), 26-28. https://www.myamericannurse.com/wp-content/uploads/2018/12/ant12-3-good-things-1207.pdf

14. Adair, K. C., Kennedy, L. A., & Sexton, B. J. (2020). Three good tools: Positively reflecting backwards and forwards is associated with robust improvements in well-being across three distinct interventions. *The Journal of Positive Psychology, 15*(5), 613-622. https://www.tandfonline.com/doi/full/10.1080/17439760.2020.1789707

CHAPTER 7

1. Clark, T. R. (2020). *The 4 stages of psychological safety: Defining a path to inclusion and innovation* (p. 99). Berrett-Koehler Publishers.

2. Garmston, R., & Wellman, B. (1999). *The adaptive school: A sourcebook for developing collaborative groups.* Christopher-Gordon.

3. Center for Leadership & Educational Equity. (1992). *Tuning protocol.* https://www.schoolreforminitiative.org/download/tuning-protocol/?wpdmdl=12767&refresh=65b0b08b899251706078347

4. Baron, D. (n.d.). *A consensus based decision-making making process.* Center for Leadership & Educational Equity. https://www.schoolreforminitiative.org/download/consensus-based-decision-making-process/?wpdmdl=12460&refresh=65b0b3ade77711706079149

5. Edmondson, A. (2014, May 4). *Building a psychologically safe workplace* [Video]. TEDx Talks. https://www.youtube.com/watch?v=LhoLuui9gX8

6. Rosenberg, M. (2015). *Nonviolent communication: A language of life* (3rd ed.). PuddleDancer Press

7. Karpman, S. (2014). *A game free life. The definitive book on the drama triangle and compassion triangle by the originator and author. The new transactional analysis of intimacy, openness, and happiness.* Drama Triangle Publications.

8. Emerald, D. (2015). *The power of TED: The empowerment dynamic* (3rd ed.). Polaris Publishing.

9. Toussaint, L. L., Shields, G. S., & Slavich, G. M. (2016). Forgiveness, stress, and health: A 5-week dynamic parallel process study. *Annals of Behavioral Medicine 50*, 727–735. https://doi.org/10.1007/s12160-016-9796-6

10. Toussaint, L., Worthington, E. L., Jr., Van Tongeren, D. R., Hook, J., Berry, J. W., Shiny, V. A., Miller, A. J., & Davis, D. E. (2018, January). *American Journal of Health Promotion*, *32*(1), 59–67. https://doi.org/10.1177/0890117116662312

CHAPTER 8

1. Center for Leadership & Educational Equity. (1992). *Tuning protocol.* https://www.schoolreforminitiative.org/download/tuning-protocol/?wpdmdl=12767&refresh=65b0b08b899251706078347

2. Tschannen-Moran, M. (n.d.). Collective teacher beliefs scale. https://wmit-pages-prod.s3.amazonaws.com/wp-content/uploads/sites/102/2021/11/01165558/Collective-Teacher-Beliefs-Scale.pdf

INDEX

CORWIN

Keep Learning...

More from **Ricky Robertson**

Building Resilience in Students Impacted by Adverse Childhood Experiences

A Whole-Staff Approach
By Victoria E. Romero, Ricky Robertson, and Amber Warner

Use trauma-informed strategies to give students the skills and support they need to succeed in school and life.

Discover how to mplement whole-school change to establish a healthy social-emotional climate for students impacted by adverse childhood experiences and the staff who support them.

Order your copy at corwin.com

CONSULTING AVAILABLE

Teach for Trust is a movement to restore, repair, and transform education, one relationship at a time. Ricky provides coaching, consultation, and multi-day professional development workshops to build systems of support for students impacted by adverse childhood experiences (ACEs) and trauma and the educators who work with them.

For more information about Ricky's coaching and consulting services visit: teachfortrust.com

Ricky Robertson

SEL241098014

Zeitfracht Medien GmbH
Ferdinand-Jühlke-Straße 7
99095 Erfurt, Deutschland
produktsicherheit@kolibri360.de